MARIAH
CAREY
REVISITED

MARIAH CAREY REVISITED

HER STORY

CHRIS NICKSON

St. Martin's Griffin
New York

Library of Congress Cataloging-in-Publication Data

Nickson, Chris.
    Mariah Carey revisited   /   by Chris Nickson.
        p.   cm.
    ISBN 0-312-19512-5
    1. Carey, Mariah.   2. Singers—United States—Biography.
    I. Title.
ML420.C2555N52   1998
782.42164'092—dc21
    [b]   98-23938
                                            CIP
                                          MN

First St. Martin's Griffin Edition: October 1998

10 9 8 7 6 5 4 3 2

For my parents,

Ray and Betty Nickson,

with all my love and gratitude,

and for **Linda,** my love, my wife.

ACKNOWLEDGMENTS

I t's been almost four years since I first sat down to write about Mariah Carey; time passes quickly. My constant thanks go to Madeleine Morel, surely one of the supreme agents, and to Jim Fitzgerald, who believed in the first book and in this revision. I'm grateful that Dave Thompson originally set me on this path. And then there are friends and colleagues whose support has been constant: Mike Murtagh, Dennis Wilken, Thom Atkinson, Paul Clark, and families Hornberg, Nagel, and Watkins. And these days anything would be unthinkable without Graham, who wasn't here the first time around.

Things were made much easier by the following articles: "From Big Dreams to the Big Time" by James Kindall, in *New York Newsday;* "How Sweet It Is" by Steve Dougherty, in *People;* Stephen Holden's pieces about Mariah in *The New York Times;* Lynn Norment's article in *Ebony,* April 1994; "Butterflies Aren't Free" by Degen Pener, *Entertainment Weekly,* September 26, 1997; "Cinderella Story" by Elysa Gardner, *Vibe,* April 1996; "Calling the Shots, Solo" by Elysa Gardner, *Los Angeles Times,* 1997.

Chris Nickson

INTRODUCTION

"I mean, it really is like Cinderella." That was how Mariah Carey described her career in 1994, and it was quite true. In place of the glass slipper was the demo tape that Columbia chief Tommy Mottola had plucked from her hand at a party. Listening to it on the way home, he'd told his driver to turn around so he could find this mysterious singer. But she was gone.

Tracking Mariah down proved easier than finding Cinderella, and the happily-ever-after part came quickly—her first five singles all reached number 1, her albums sold in the millions, and in 1993, in a picture-book ceremony, she married the man who'd discovered her.

Everything seemed perfect. The hits kept on coming. If there was one truly popular artist of the nineties, it was Mariah. Every new release seemed to set a new record: the first female solo artist to have a single enter the *Billboard* Hot 100 at number 1, the first person to achieve that twice, the longest-running number 1, the best-selling recording artist in the world. Her successes just kept coming and coming.

But even fairy tales have their dark side. On May 30, 1997, Mariah Carey and Tommy Mottola officially announced their separation. Their marriage was, to all intents and purposes, over.

It was a sad and difficult time. Mariah was in the middle of working on her new album, *Butterfly.* Having achieved the security that had been missing all throughout her childhood—a house that was hers, money, even fame—she was now back on her own.

But the woman who was in the recording studio during the

first half of 1997 wasn't the same little girl who'd been discovered in November 1988. She'd grown and matured, and was well on the road to truly finding herself. And she proved it on *Butterfly,* releasing her most accomplished record yet, one that put her exactly where she wanted to be—quite firmly in the middle of R&B territory, with credibility in the street and on the radio. Once again, there was a happy ending.

WHATEVER THE MAGIC ingredient is that makes a star, some mixture of talent, charisma, and luck, Mariah has it. From her very first record, she's had the golden touch that has made everything she's issued into a big hit. And it's all the more remarkable when you consider that she's had a hand in writing and shaping the arrangement of virtually every song she's recorded. She's even been the coproducer of most of them. Her involvement has been very different from that of the other big-name female singers. Each record is *hers,* from its conception to its release.

But that was the dream she always had. From the time she was a child, she knew singing was her destiny. Her mother was a singer. Mariah loved music, and she had been born with a remarkable vocal gift, but all too often childish dreams get put away later. Not for Mariah. She *knew.* She believed.

She's a woman who spent a lot of years on the outside. Her mixed-race heritage—Irish, Venezuelan, and African American—meant that she didn't quite fit in anywhere when she was growing up. Music was her comfort then, the place where she could disappear and forget the insults she heard in the real world.

Music was always there for her when she needed it. In many ways, it has provided the basis for the relationships in her life. Her mother gave her voice lessons. In Ben Margulies, she met another struggling musician and songwriter; the pooling of their talents, and their friendship, helped Mariah toward the big time. With Walter Afanasieff, the man who's coproduced and cowritten so much material with her, she's built a trust over seven years.

And it was music, really, that forged the link between Tommy and her.

Simply put, music has been Mariah's life. As she's grown, her music has grown with her. Even if each of her albums didn't sell in the millions, she'd still be doing it, recording, writing, singing. Music defines her as a person. Through each of her albums, you can see her growing, from the rather tentative girl of *Mariah Carey,* who felt the need to impress by showing what the high end of her voice could do, to the self-assured songstress of *Butterfly,* who still had anxieties, but whose voice could now curl around a lyric, and who no longer needed gimmicks to prove anything about her worth.

No one, quite literally no one, has done what Mariah Carey has. Exploding out of nowhere, it seemed, her success was without precedent. Those female pop stars who'd gone before her—Madonna, Whitney Houston—needed to look to their laurels. It wasn't a competition, but Mariah beat them anyway, selling more records, having more number 1 hits, staying at the top of the charts longer.

Mariah was different. She didn't need to keep reinventing herself, like Madonna. And, unlike Whitney's music, Mariah's didn't veer more and more to the middle of the road. Quite the opposite. Beginning with "Dreamlover" on *Music Box,* the R&B element grew stronger and stronger. It had always been there, a vital part of who she was, even on *Mariah Carey,* which won several R&B awards. Now it was quite overt in its progression to "Fantasy," then to "Honey," which was a contemporary—thanks in part to a production by Sean ("Puffy") Combs—as anything on the market. It was real. And so was Mariah.

Not that she was about to ditch the ballads. She still loved them. But even they were more R&B now, real slow jams, sexy, purring. She was exactly where she wanted to be, in a place where her heart, her mind, and her voice all came together.

* * *

MARIAH'S STORY WAS, in so many ways, rags-to-riches, perfectly American. After her parents divorced, she and her mother had moved around Manhattan and Long Island more than a dozen times, sometimes being forced to stay with friends because they had no place of their own. And after she graduated from high school and moved out to find her fame and fortune, Mariah really did live on next to nothing, with just one pair of holey sneakers to her name, making a pan of macaroni and cheese last for days. From there to what she possesses now was a long journey. Maybe not in years, but in other ways. It's a story that manages to be both inspiring and inspirational. It's a story of how belief in yourself and your abilities really can pay off.

And with every success comes responsibility, something Mariah understands all too well. That's why she's become a staunch supporter of the Fresh Air Fund, an organization that helps underprivileged kids in New York—kids like the one she once was—taking them to camp, encouraging them. Between a benefit concert, other work, and her own donations, she's raised more than a million dollars for the Fund, which named one of its camps in her honor. It's a place where Mariah goes to talk to the kids about the music business and about believing in themselves.

Predicting the future is always a tricky business, but one thing that seems certain is that Mariah's star won't be fading anytime soon. She continues to go from strength to strength as she develops. These days, her music has muscle; it moves. Mariah's a highly talented writer who has her finger on the popular pulse, a producer who understands how to bring out the best in herself. She has her own label, releasing music by other people that she believes in, giving them the chance she had to struggle for herself. And now she's also an actress, with a movie in the works, which just might prove to be the start of yet another career for her.

Mariah's the Voice of the Nineties, someone who can do it all, who has the golden touch in her music. And even if her personal life hasn't been a case of living happily ever after with her Prince

Charming, she's coming through that, into herself, a woman of the nineties overcoming adversity.

That's now. But what about the past? Who is she? Where did she come from? How did she become a huge star so quickly? What is it that makes her music so special? And what makes Mariah Carey tick?

1

Patricia Hickey was born with a wondrous gift. She could sing, not just the way many people can, carrying a tune or warbling in the shower, but with a rare clarity that promised a future in music. The daughter of Irish immigrants from County Cork, she grew up in the Midwest never knowing her father, who died a month before she was born. He had been a singer himself, and a musician, and while he could not be there to witness his little girl's growth, he was at least able to bequeath her his talent.

At the age of seventeen, Patricia went to New York and won a place with the New York City Opera. It was still a young company, organized in 1943 during World War II as part of the City Center of Music and Drama. Its mission was to provide good opera at affordable prices. It quickly acquired a reputation for both the quality and range of its productions, as it began to offer premieres of new American works as well as revivals of classical pieces.

By 1960, Patricia Hickey had become Patricia Carey, after marrying Alfred Roy Carey, an aeronautical engineer of African American and Venezuelan descent, and the couple were soon parents of a son, Morgan. A year later, he would be joined by a sister, Alison. But it was a union, sadly, that would estrange Patricia—and her children, including Mariah—from her disapproving family.

"My mother's family basically disowned her when she married my father," Mariah explained in *Smash Hits*. "So later I was like, 'Well, where does this leave me? Am I a bad person?' You know. It's not that common still to be a multiracial person, but I'm happy with the combination of things that I am."

Alfred and Patricia moved from one all-white suburb on New York's Long Island to another, encountering a tremendous amount of prejudice and harassment as an interracial couple, a pairing that was not so common in those days, and one which tended to generate extreme reactions. "They went through some very hard times before I was born," Mariah told *People* magazine. "They had their dogs poisoned, their cars set on fire and blown up." Not unnaturally, these events caused many problems. "It put a strain on their relationship. There was always this tension. They just fought all the time."

But by the late sixties, Patricia was at last achieving some success in the operatic world. Still with the New York City Opera, the mezzo-soprano had become a soloist in the company, working with such world-famous performers as Beverly Sills.

Then, in the fall of 1969, Patricia discovered she was pregnant again. And on March 27, 1970, Mariah Carey was born.

The world she entered was a violent place. Fighting was going on in the Middle East. The conflict in Vietnam continued, claiming thousands of lives—indeed, a few weeks after Mariah's birth, a war protest at Kent State University in Ohio would result in the deaths of four students, shot by the Ohio National Guard. But at the same time, ironically, Simon and Garfunkel's gentle, hopeful "Bridge Over Troubled Water" was number 1 on the *Billboard* Hot 100, enjoying a six-week run in that position.

Although Mariah once jokingly stated, "I think my mother chose the name Mariah because it would be a stage name," Patricia actually took the name from the song "They Call the Wind Mariah," featured in the Lerner and Lowe musical *Paint Your Wagon,* which, as a film, was enjoying great popularity in 1970. (A song from the movie, "Wand'rin Star," sung by Lee Marvin, was number 1 in England the day Mariah was born.)

The family, sadly, continued to be the target of rampant racial intolerance, and the ongoing problems it caused in the relationship between Alfred and Patricia proved insurmountable, causing their separation and divorce, which occurred when Mariah was three.

Recalled Mariah, "That made me feel very anti-marriage. I thought that I'd never marry."

One of Mariah's earliest memories, unsurprisingly, involved singing, but also showed the problems that existed within the family. "My father was very strict, one of the strictest disciplinarians, and there was this whole dinner-table etiquette; everybody spoke only when spoken to, and so on. And I was a more free spirit; my mom kind of shielded me from that. And I loved singing; I was singing since I started talking. . . . So I was singing at the table . . . and my father said, 'There will be *no singing* at the table!' So I got up from the table, and I went into the living room, and I got on the coffee table and continued singing at the top of my lungs."

After the divorce, Alison lived with her father, while Morgan, just in his teens, and Mariah lived with their mother. At first they saw their father weekly, but those visits, although amicable, soon became less frequent. "My father and I had a good relationship for a minute there, right after the divorce," Mariah recalled. "Everybody wishes they had a 'Brady Bunch' family, but it's not reality.

"He's a good person," she elaborated. "I don't have anything against him. It's just very difficult growing up in a divorced family—the tension, anger, and bitterness between the parents is often put off on the children, and because I was so young when they divorced, it was a *major* split for me." She discovered, in her visits with her father, that they really had very little in common. His talents as a mathematician weren't passed on to his younger daughter, and he didn't share her love of music. However, Mariah did retain some fond memories of the time they spent together when she was young. Alfred Carey eventually took a job in Washington, D.C., and moved there, but continued also to maintain a home on Long Island.

For all the problems, conflicts, and arguments between Patricia and Alfred, Patricia never tried to turn the children against their father. Mariah recounted, "[L]ucky for me, my mother never said anything negative about my father. She never discouraged me from having a good feeling about him. She always taught me to believe in myself, to love all the things I am. In that sense I'm very lucky, because I could have been a very screwed-up person."

By 1972, Patricia had discovered that her younger daughter had inherited her singing talent. It happened as Patricia was rehearsing at home for her debut as Maddalena in Verdi's opera, *Rigoletto.*

"I missed my cue," she explained, "but Mariah didn't. She sang it—in Italian—at exactly the right point. She wasn't yet three."

Once Mariah had found she possessed this ability, she used it constantly. She walked around the house "like a little tape recorder, and I'd mimic whatever I heard, whether it was my brother's or sister's records, or whatever songs were on the radio at the time." What she heard mostly, though, was her mother's voice. Patricia was still with the New York City Opera, and would often rehearse her roles at home. Little Mariah would sit next to her, correct her errors in pitch, and sing along—in Italian.

Music was always around the Carey house. The newly single Patricia had a difficult time making ends meet. Her position at the opera didn't offer enough money, so she became a freelance vocal coach. She happily encouraged Mariah's musical precociousness. "I grew up on my own with my mom," Mariah said. "I was always singing around the house because *she* was always singing, so I would try to mimic her. She couldn't shut me up. She wouldn't let anybody baby-talk around me. She had me around all her friends as a kid, and she used to say I was like a little adult. All I wanted to do was sing for my mom's friends, so I would memorize every jingle on TV and whatever records were playing around the house, like Stevie Wonder, Aretha Franklin."

When Mariah was four, although she was considered a "born singer," her mother started giving her voice lessons; the raw ability was obviously there, but she needed training to learn how to use and develop it properly, and only formal study would give her that. This shared talent—and time—reinforced the bond between Mariah and Patricia, in a family that was always financially on the brink. "I grew up without having a lot of things, money and stuff like that. My mother and I moved around a lot; she worked three jobs sometimes. I went through a lot of rough times when I was a little girl." A lack of money creates constant strain and strife, a vicious cycle of near poverty, and most certainly a sense of living on the edge. Everything that comes into the house immediately goes out again to cover bills; there's no chance to save or to get ahead, no sense of security, just a feeling of always struggling.

And they did struggle. Over the course of fourteen years, Patricia and Mariah would move thirteen times in the New York area, sometimes even staying with friends, as Patricia sought work in her field.

"There were times we didn't have a place to live," Mariah would recall. "Those were very frightening periods."

But Patricia was always there for her daughter, encouraging and supporting her. It's her mother, Mariah said, "who is most responsible for me having the courage to be able to do what I'm doing." Patricia took great pains to install a strong, healthy sense of self-esteem in her daughter and to reinforce the idea of the girl's talent. It was a spark, Mariah was certain, that gave her the strength to become a professional singer.

Patricia's work wasn't limited to daytime hours. Singers often perform long into the night, and vocal coaches frequently work in the evenings. Whenever possible, she would take Mariah with her, but frequently that wouldn't be feasible. "My mom and I almost grew up together," Mariah said. Being together so much made them almost seem like a team, and being around adults caused Mariah to grow up quickly, a trait that was extremely useful on those occasions when her mother had to work at night and Mariah had to stay home alone, with only the radio as a babysitter.

"I used to take the radio, steal the radio from the kitchen and listen to it under the covers and sing all night. That's when I was beginning my insomniac days back when I was like four and [it] hasn't gone away."

Even then, she knew she wanted to be a singer.

"[I]t's something I've always wanted to do. . . . Since I knew there was such a thing as what you do for a living, I knew I wanted to be a singer. . . . [My mother] didn't persuade me to do it, but she was a professional singer . . . when I was a little girl so I guess it wouldn't be such a farfetched thing as it would be for some people . . . you know, to dream of doing it."

Her mother might have encouraged her, but not everyone was so enthusiastic. "I told one teacher that I wanted to be a singer and was told, 'There are millions of people out there who can sing. What makes you any different? Don't get your hopes up.' I couldn't believe a teacher would actually say that to someone who had a dream."

It was during this time that Mariah made her real singing debut. In 1976, as a first-grader, she was chosen for a high-school production of the musical *South Pacific,* in which she soloed on the tune "Honey Bun."

Her musical education was continuing, too, in more ways than one. Patricia's friends would visit, and everything from the late jazz singer Billie Holiday to opera would be played.

"I was singing with my mom and her musician friends from the time I was about four years old. I'd get home from school, and she would have, like, five friends over who were jazz musicians, and I'd end up singing 'My Funny Valentine' at two in the morning."

Mariah was also encouraged to take piano lessons to complement the voice training, but, by her own admission, she was "lazy"; it's something she now regrets. "When I was little, my mom tried to get me to do piano, but I said, 'This comes naturally, I can do it by ear, I don't want to learn.' I should have taken lessons because it would be easier for me now. . . . Sometimes ideas just come, and because I'm worrying about trying to find the chords, I end up losing part of the idea."

There was also the soul music that Morgan loved (and Alison, too, when she visited), in particular Stevie Wonder. He would continue to be an inspiration to Mariah, as would another singer popular at the time, Minnie Ripperton.

"I remember hearing her song, 'Loving You,' all the time and trying to hit the high notes on it. I never could—for a while. I guess it was just a great ambition of mine to use my voice in that way. . . . I started to find old records of hers and listen to her style. I just thought it was an incredible gift that she had."

Mariah started out mimicking it all as an infant, then grew to love it herself, which would lead her to one of the joys of her life, along with hip-hop—gospel music.

So many of the soul singers that Morgan listened to had grown up singing in the Baptist church—Al Green, Aretha Franklin (whose father was a famous preacher), Stevie Wonder, Gladys Knight—and it showed in the way they approached their music. Once Mariah discovered that two of her idols, Al Green and Aretha Franklin, had both recorded gospel albums, she went out and bought them.

It proved to be a major turning point for her, and very soon she was investigating other gospel artists who hadn't made any secular records, people like Shirley Caesar, the Clark Sisters, Mahalia Jackson, and Vanessa Bell Armstrong. The rawness and freedom of the voices touched a chord in the girl, one that would continue to resonate inside her, to influence and motivate her. Along with pop and R&B, she continues to love gospel, and admitted that there was a time she bought gospel tapes from late-night television. And the influence has frequently shown up in her music, whether it be in the soaring arrangement of the backing vocals, or the way a piano is played, or the rich tones of her own voice.

Mariah's introduction to this kind of music had come on the sporadic visits she made to her father's mother, whom Mariah would accompany to the Baptist church where she would hear traditional spirituals. These were the only times during her childhood that Mariah was able to experience the sensation of being part of a large family. Unfortunately, the visits were rare. "I wish I had been part of it more," she said.

One of the other big musical influences as she grew up was rap, right from the time the first Sugar Hill Gang single hit the radio in 1979, when Mariah was nine years old. "I grew up in New York," she pointed out. "I've been listening to urban music, hip-hop, since it was invented," and she'd go on later to feel that she shared a lot with people who worked in those fields. "I went through a lot and saw a lot of things, my life was far from sheltered or privileged, so when I work with urban acts, people who have come up from the streets and worked hard to get where they are, I feel as if we have a lot in common."

MARIAH NEVER HAD any choice but to be well aware of her racial background. It was something that definitely added to the problems she felt as a child. "It's been difficult for me," she explained in an interview with *Ebony,* "moving around so much, having to grow up by myself . . . my parents divorced. And I always felt kind of different from everyone else in my neighborhoods. I was a different person ethnically. And sometimes that can be a problem. If you look a certain way, everybody goes, 'White girl,' and I'd go, 'No, that's not what I am.' " But while the brief time she spent with her grandmother had served to make her very aware of her black heritage, she knew she wasn't completely black, either. She felt it upset people that she refused to come out and state she was one or the other. However, it was impossible to do without denying a big part of herself. To call herself black would ignore her completely Irish mother ("my best friend"). At the same time, saying she was "black, Venezuelan, and Irish" satisfied no one; it appeared to be too much of a compromise. For Mariah, though, it was all she could do, because it was the truth, and because it brought home to her the ultimate difficulty in being an interracial child—being neither one thing nor the other. So she defined herself in the only possible way: "I am a human being, a person."

All three of the Carey children found themselves on the receiving end of prejudice. Alison had the darkest skin in the family, and when she was young, the neighborhood kids would single her out. "They'd shout racial slurs and beat her up," Mariah said in a mixture of sadness and anger. "Then my brother would go in and fight for her. . . . It was tough."

But when she was down and gloomy, Mariah could always disappear into her music. Where other kids might stand in the driveway and shoot baskets, she would walk alone in the woods, or anywhere she could be by herself, and let her voice ring.

Mariah was also finding another way of expressing herself—writing poetry, although it didn't always go over well in class. In a manner that's unfortunately all too common in schools, when she handed in her poetry assignment, her third-grade teacher, Mr. Cohen, refused to believe she could have done the work herself, and accused her of copying the lines from a book.

But at home there would always be that best friend, her mother, "the mainstay in my life," ready with all the comfort and support she could muster.

"Growing up, it was difficult for me to find people that I connected with because of all my issues of feeling separate and apart."

She felt like an outsider, someone who didn't belong, not just because of her background and lack of money, but also because of her appearance. "When I was in seventh grade, I was an ugly duckling. I had really hairy eyebrows and I didn't know that you were supposed to pluck them. So I started shaving off bits of my eyebrows. Pretty soon, there were none left. Then I picked up this hair stuff called 'Golden Blond.' I put it on my hair and started drying it with this bright orange blow dryer. The next thing I knew, my hair was the same color as the blow dryer. Of course, the second I left the house, I ran into this kid I was totally in love with and he said, 'What happened to you?' "

FINALLY, AFTER TOO many unstable years, constantly struggling and moving, the Careys managed to establish a place of their own. When Mariah was a teenager, she and her mother were able to settle in one place for longer than a few months. On Long Island, they had an unassuming house in an affluent neighborhood of Huntington Bay, which, an unnamed friend said, "might have been tough on her"—a reference to their monetary situation. "I never had any financial security," Mariah said, recalling her childhood. "I dreamed of possessing things. Lucky for me I had my music to hold on to as a goal. It was like, 'These people may not think I'm as good as them, but I can *sing!*' "

By the time Mariah entered Greenlawn's Harborfields High School, she was already writing songs, something she'd begun in junior high, and by the age of fourteen she already had an after-school job as a singer on demonstration records at a few local Long Island studios. These were her very first professional steps toward realizing her dream of singing and writing music for a living. As her school friend Patricia Johnson told *New York Newsday,* from seventh grade on, Mariah had been openly telling people exactly what she wanted to do with her life. "And she always did what she said she was going to do."

And she insisted on not being pushed around. At one time, Mariah had a problem with some older girls in the neighborhood "who were really mean to me." They moved away, and Mariah was able to get their new phone number. She then got her revenge with prank phone calls. In the end, however, it all backfired; the calls were traced, the police talked to Patricia, and "I had to pay for the calls out of my allowance."

Patricia was still giving her daughter vocal training, working to bring to fruition the talent Mariah had shown as a little girl. She was careful, though, not to impose the values of her own classical training on her daughter. "[S]he's never been a pushy mom. She never said, 'Give it more of an operatic feel.' I respect opera like crazy but it didn't influence me." Indeed, although she knew and greatly respected the technical ability involved in opera, the music never touched her, and she had no desire to subject herself to the endless years of training necessary to become a diva or a prima donna.

At Harborfields High, Mariah didn't publicly display her ability. Quite deliberately, she didn't join any of the school choirs or take part in any talent shows.

"I thought I was too cool to do anything related to school activities," she told *Vibe*. "I thought I was the tough chick of the school. But I think that stemmed from being insecure as a kid."

Really, her music was still a very private, personal thing, and that was the way she wished to keep it. But otherwise she was a perfectly normal student—outgoing, popular, and outwardly full of self-confidence, which earned her the nickname "Miss Mod."

"I'd hang out with my friends," she reminisced, "and go to parties, and just be stupid and goof off, but when I was at home, I was listening to music and writing songs." And in comparing her conversation with that of her friends, her focus becomes quite evident: "Girls grow up constantly talking about having babies. I talked about music."

By now she had a writing partner, a friend, Gavin Christopher, and the songs they were producing so impressed Morgan Carey that for his little sister's sixteenth birthday, he paid for her to make her own demo tape in a professional twenty-four-track studio in Manhattan. "We needed someone to play keyboards for a song. . . ." Mariah explained to Fred Bronson in the *Billboard Book of Number One Hits*. "We called someone and he couldn't come, so by accident we stumbled upon Ben [Margulies]. Ben came to the session, and he can't really play keyboards very well—he's really more of a drummer—but after that day, we kept in touch, and we sort of clicked as writers."

That comment was a great understatement; the pair would go on to achieve the incredible success of the *Mariah Carey* album. But that time was still a long way off. For now, they would have to be content with perfecting their craft, writing songs, and laying the groundwork for their future.

Ben's father owned a cabinet factory, Bedworks, in the Chelsea area of Manhattan, and he'd allowed his son to set up a studio in the back room there. So it was to Bedworks that Mariah began commuting—with her mother's permission—on a regular basis, often staying out until two in the morning. Trying to juggle school, music, and sleep, it was inevitable that something would suffer. So it was perhaps no big surprise that around this time Mariah's nickname changed to "Mirage," indicating her frequent absences from school.

The duo quickly began completing material. The first song they wrote and recorded together was called "Here We Go Round Again." It was a tune with a great deal of Motown influence. Ben created the music; Mariah wrote the lyrics. As they listened to the completed tape in the tiny studio behind the wood shop, the excitement grew. It didn't just sound good—it sounded *incredible!* And so a partnership was born.

But still Mariah kept quiet at school about her ambitions, at least until she was called upon to explain why her schoolwork was so mediocre. Harborfields assistant principal John Garvey explained, "When you talked to her about it, she'd let you know it just wasn't that important in her life because she was going to be a rock star. She was fully convinced it was going to happen. Nothing was going to stand in her way. You could talk to her until you were blue in the face, and it didn't do any good."

Mariah didn't view things in quite the same way. To her, all this nagging meant a lack of support for her dream. The teachers picked on her because she didn't want to follow the conventional track. She had no desire to pass math and get into a good college—or any college, for that matter. She didn't need it. It didn't matter. She was going to be a singer.

"What they used to write in my report card was, 'She's very smart, but she doesn't apply herself unless it's something she likes.' Which was, like, creative writing. I was always in the classes with the smart kids. The honors Creative Writing class. Then I would be in the worst remedial math. I hated math."

One person who did offer Mariah some support was her high-school guidance counselor, James Malone. He encouraged her to follow her dreams, but suggested that she develop other skills, in case, like so many, her dreams never came true.

And some of his advice was taken to heart. In her last two years of high school, Mariah studied beauty—cosmetics, skin, and hair. "I did five hundred hours of beauty school. I knew I wanted to be a singer, but I figured I would like to have something to fall back on, you know?"

Malone even told her that if singing didn't work out for her, she was always welcome to return to him, and he'd offer whatever advice he could on a career path. "You know," he mused in 1991, "I don't think she's going to need that counseling now."

No matter how focused Mariah was on singing, in at least one area the teenager in her shone through—her room was always messy. And, of course, Patricia would wonder how she'd manage when she was eventually living alone and had to clean up after herself. "Well, I'm going to be a famous singer and have a maid," was Mariah's half-joking response.

Although working hard to support her family, Patricia had not put her personal life entirely on hold. She'd met a man, Joseph Vian, and fallen in love, and in 1987, while Mariah was in her senior year of high school, Patricia and Joseph married. Sadly, it wasn't destined to last; the divorce between the couple became final in 1992.

Perhaps to the astonishment of a few of the teachers who'd found her attitude toward classes incomprehensible, Mariah graduated from Harborfields High School with the Class of 1987. In her senior yearbook, she listed her likes as "sleeping late" (not too surprising, all things considered), "Corvettes," and "guiedos" [sic]— Italian men.

Then, within a few days, as if it couldn't happen fast enough, she'd packed all her stuffed animals, posters, tapes, and clothes, and she'd moved to Manhattan. Mariah was looking for the Big Time.

2

So, at seventeen (the same age her mother had been when she moved there), Mariah was living in New York City, trying everything she could think of to make her dream come true. She had a place to live, a one-bedroom loft she shared with two other girls who also aspired to be performers. It was, to say the least, a cramped existence. Mariah slept on a mattress on the floor of the living room. None of them had any money for more than the basic necessities, to the point that sometimes eating would be classified as a luxury. More than once, the roommates stretched out a box of macaroni-and-cheese over the course of a week.

"Three months before I got my record deal," Mariah recalled, "I was having a bagel a day and Snapple ice tea drink. My friend and I would go to the deli and beg this guy to give us some Snapples."

All Mariah's free time was spent pursuing her musical goal. She went, on foot, to virtually every record company in town, carrying the demo tape she and Ben had made. But, as she explained in an interview with the *Chicago Tribune,* "For . . . a year I couldn't pay someone to listen to my tapes. They think if you don't have a high-powered manager or don't have a record company that's already interested in you, you're no good. I had no connections and I was running with my writing partner, who was also new and didn't have any connections, either."

It was a very frustrating situation, one encountered by any number of new artists. All they have to keep themselves going is their music and a large amount of faith. Ben's studio didn't have any more than basic equipment. But he was sure their demos sounded good. And he never had any doubts about Mariah's exceptional talent, as he was happy to tell: "She had the ability just to hear things in the air and to start developing songs out of them. Often I would sit down and start playing something, and from the feel of a chord, she would start singing melody lines and coming up with a concept."

But, apart from the time spent recording at Bedworks with Ben, or trying to get a foot in the door with a record company, Mariah also had to earn a living. To do that, she held a series of jobs, most of which she lost because she had "an attitude." It was all work of the "easy come, easy go" variety. She hatchecked in clubs, and hostessed and waitressed at restaurants like the Sports Bar and the Boathouse Cafe in Central Park. But none of it paid her a living wage. She had (and has kept as a reminder of those days) one pair of sneakers, black lace-ups that had originally belonged to her mother. "They were the only shoes I owned. They were literally falling apart and caused hell for my feet in winter. . . . My idea of heaven was a decent pair of shoes." There was no choice but to wear them every day, even during winter's worst wet slush and snow. Then, at home, if they were lucky, there was a single plate of pasta to split between the three girls.

Mariah didn't care in the least about her jobs; they weren't her future. Music was her obsession. Even at work, it filled her mind. "I'd be sitting there watching some video—Debbie Gibson or something—and I'd be fuming furiously. Like, 'Why do I have to sit here and waitress while these people are doing videos?' "

All too often she'd be discovered, after much fruitless searching and yelling, sitting with a pair of headphones cutting off the outside world, singing along to a tune and working on a set of lyrics for a new song, when she should have been looking after customers. And, almost invariably, that would mean the end of another job.

"I was a really, really bad waitress," she admitted. "I would forget things, and I really wasn't into it, so I wasn't that nice to the customers. You have to be overly nice to get a good tip, and I wasn't like that, so they ended up firing me."

Out of this awful procession of labor, there was one position that stuck in her mind as being without question the *very* worst. For two days, she swept up the cut hair in a salon owned by a man who liked to give his employees nicknames like "Lightning" and "Electricity," which were displayed on plaques above their stations. While this struck Mariah as strange, she didn't pay it too much mind until the owner—after repeatedly staring at her and asking her name—announced that from then on she would be known as "Echo." When she asked why, he explained that when someone worked in his salon, he named them. Needless to say, that didn't sit well with Mariah. In fact, she quit on the spot. There was always another job, and it had to be better than that one.

Being young, Mariah could push herself to the limit, and she did. Every day she worked, waitressing—or at whatever her job was that week—until midnight. As soon as her shift was over, she'd join Ben down at Bedworks on Nineteenth Street and work until 7 A.M., when she'd go home and sleep until it was time to get up for work again. Almost her only break from the routine came when she'd make another round of the record companies.

But there was never any doubt in Mariah's mind as to why she was putting herself through such misery—she was certain of what the future would hold: "I was doing all that because I wanted to get a record deal and make an album. I can do things that aren't productive or I can make an album."

After several months of menial jobs, things did begin to look up. Mariah had become friendly with a number of musicians, one of whom played drums for an R&B singer named Brenda K. Starr. He mentioned that one of Brenda's backup singers had recently quit, and suggested to Mariah that she apply for the job. "I really didn't want to do it," she told Fred Bronson, "but I said it's gotta be better than what I'm doing now. So I went to the audition, and Brenda was such a great person."

The range and fluidity of Mariah's voice impressed her prospective employer, and suddenly she was realizing a little bit of her dream—she was making some of her living from singing. Unfortunately, it was only a part-time gig; Brenda wasn't a big star, so she couldn't afford to keep musicians and singers on a permanent payroll. But it was a start.

This new job didn't do much to improve Mariah's finances. She still had to wear the same holey sneakers, and she always seemed to be dressed in a single outfit that consisted of a short jacket and a pair of black stretch pants, no matter how bitter the New York winter weather. In fact, it reached the point where Starr began to worry that her new backup singer might end up catching pneumonia in such thin clothes.

Brenda had a record contract with CBS Epic, (for whose big-sister label, Columbia, Mariah would soon be recording herself), which at this stage put her ahead of Mariah. She would release an album, *Brenda K. Starr,* on MCA, and *By Heart* on Epic in 1991, as well as contribute to three soundtracks: *License to Drive, She's Out of Control,* and *George LaMond: Bad of the Heart.* Although Mariah never recorded as a part of Brenda's band, she did participate in a number of live shows with her, and over the course of their time together, the two became good friends. Sometimes, when there were no gigs scheduled and Mariah wasn't working on her own material, the two would spend an evening sitting and chatting. Neither had grown up with a father, and it was a subject that still rankled them both.

The friendship between the two quickly grew by leaps and bounds, and Brenda recognized and happily acknowledged Mariah's unique talent. "Most singers would have said, 'Stay in the background and don't sing too loud,' " Mariah told *People.* Instead, Brenda began promoting her discovery, introducing Mariah to her contacts in the music industry. A few years later, Mariah had nothing but praise for her former boss: "She helped me out a lot. She was always, 'Here's my friend Mariah, here's her tape; she sings, writes. . . .' "

And once Mariah had achieved success, she never forgot Brenda. At one time, Starr was going through a bad patch. She was living in New Jersey, trying to get by on very little money. Christmas was coming, and things looked bleak. Out of the blue, completely unannounced, Mariah arrived, bringing a rocking horse from F. A. O. Schwarz for Brenda's daughter and an extremely expensive makeup kit for Brenda herself.

"She started laughing with the curls falling in her face," is the way Starr happily described the scene. "It was like she was Santa Claus. I started crying."

But perhaps such gifts were only appropriate. After all, if it hadn't been for the persuasiveness of Brenda K. Starr, Mariah might have ended up waiting a lot longer for her recording contract. . . .

TOMMY MOTTOLA HAD become head of CBS Columbia's U.S. organization in the spring of 1988, replacing Al Teller not long after Sony's takeover of the industry giant. It was one of the senior jobs with what was still the country's biggest record company, an extremely powerful position. A genial, bearded man, Mottola had charge of an operation that was doing well, with top-selling, established artists like Billy Joel and Barbra Streisand. However, there were problems. A competitor, Warner Bros., was rapidly increasing its share of the market, while Columbia didn't have many new acts to introduce and make money on. Changing that had to be Mottola's priority.

Born in 1952 in the Bronx, Tommy Mottola had been involved with music all his life. He studied acting and voice at Hofstra University on Long Island, and while there managed to win a recording contract with Epic (ironically, one of the Columbia labels). Under the name T. D. Valentine, he released several singles, including "Love Trap" and "A Woman Without Love." But none of them became a hit. So, armed with a degree and having been dropped by Epic, Mottola moved to the business side of the music industry, starting out as a promotion man for the large music-publishing company, Chappell Music. In his early days there, he came across Hall and Oates, at the time a struggling young band,

and eventually helped them find a record deal on Atlantic (after Epic had turned them down). Then, in 1975, he founded Champion Entertainment with Sandy Linzer, a former Epic staff producer, and began managing not only Hall and Oates, but also Odyssey and Dr. Buzzard's Original Savannah Band. A few years later, Champion would be handling the careers of such stars as John Mellencamp, Split Enz, and Carly Simon, and Hall and Oates would write about Mottola on their *Silver* album in the song "Gino (The Manager)."

Married with two children, for Mottola the move to Columbia was a definite step up the business ladder, but some expressed doubts about his fitness for the job. But he was well aware of his priorities: Columbia had no young female star to challenge Whitney Houston (who recorded for Arista) or Madonna (whose records appeared on Sire), and he wanted to find a pop diva for Columbia. And quickly. It could solve all the problems.

ON A CHILLY Friday night in November 1988, Brenda was trying to persuade Mariah to go with her to a music-business party for WDG Records, a label which no longer exists. Mariah wasn't crazy about socializing ("[Y]ou know I had never been around industry people or anything like that before, so it's like 'Oh man,' you know. . . ."). Her hectic work and recording schedules left her tired, and besides, clubs and parties always tended to be smoky, which aggravated her throat. But Brenda insisted. It was Friday night; they needed a break. There'd be food there. Finally, Mariah gave in.

Several executives from CBS Columbia, Brenda's parent label, were there, including Tommy Mottola and Jerry Greenberg, a man Brenda wanted Mariah to meet. Toward the end of the evening, Mariah managed to pluck up her courage and approached Greenberg with her tape. But, even as she reached out to give it to him, another hand—Mottola's—came down and snatched it away. A few minutes later, he left the party, and so did Mariah and Brenda. It was, Mariah decided, another waste of time. She'd probably never hear anything. But at least someone at the top of the organization would listen to her demo—if he ever bothered to play it. From here, the story has more or less passed into the folklore of the music business. On his way home in his limousine, Mottola took the tape from his pocket and slipped it into the cassette deck. After hearing just two of the tape's four songs, he instructed his driver to turn around and return to the party. He looked around for the singer, but didn't see her. As if she were Cinderella, she'd vanished.

The weekend followed, a frustrating time for Mottola, who was trying to track down the elusive vocalist. He knew she'd accompanied Brenda, but that was the only thing he knew about her. As Mariah told *People,* "[The tape] didn't have my name on it. He couldn't match up the voice with this Long Island kid in a football cheerleading jacket."

But as soon as Monday arrived, Mottola was on the phone, and the search for his Cinderella proved somewhat easier than Prince Charming's. Through Brenda K. Starr's management, he was able to find Mariah's name and number, and without hesitation he called her.

"He left a message on my machine," Mariah continued. "I called back stuttering: 'Can I speak to M-mister M-Mottola?' He said, 'I think we can make hit records.' I was like freaking *out!"*

Later that same afternoon, a very nervous Mariah, accompanied by her mother Patricia, sat in the office of the president of CBS Records, U.S.

Mottola said later, "When I heard and saw Mariah, there was absolutely no doubt she was in every way destined for stardom." He'd found his baby act, his pop diva.

Coincidentally, at this time, another record label began expressing some interest in Mariah, which led to a small bidding war for her talent. But Mottola knew her potential; he wasn't about to let anyone else stand in his way. CBS had power, and he wielded it.

Within a month, in December 1988, Mariah Carey signed a contract with CBS Columbia Records. Dreams did come true.

3

Whatever Mariah might have anticipated after she signed her contract, it probably wasn't what ended up happening to her during 1989. All of a sudden, instead of waitressing, sweeping up hair, and quitting jobs to avoid being called "Echo," she was packing and repacking her suitcase as she alternated her time between long, intense sessions in recording studios on the East and West Coasts.

It was Don Ienner's idea. He was the new addition to the Columbia staff, lured over by Mottola from Arista, where he'd been a promotions man and witnessed the things that had made a star out of Whitney Houston. Which made him a natural to work with Mariah. "Tommy told me, 'She's incredible, you just won't believe how good she is.' As far as he was concerned, it was the Second Coming." And as soon as he heard her for himself, Ienner was quick to agree. He, too, saw the potential in that voice. It had the ability to cross over into every market; it was a gold mine. "For this particular time, she is my number one priority," he told *Rolling Stone,* adding with a remarkable degree of honesty, "We don't look at her as a dance-pop artist. We look at her as a franchise."

And that meant the label wasn't about to take any chances. Ienner selected a group of star producers, men with long, proven track records of hits. There was Ric Wake, an Anglo-American whose most recent success had been with such names as: dance artist Taylor Dayne; Rhett Lawrence, who had an extensive history of working with acts like Earth, Wind, and Fire; Smokey Robinson, perhaps the king of the soul balladeers; and Epic's strongest act by far, Michael Jackson. And then there was Narada

Michael Walden, one of the hottest talents behind the mixing board. His credits filled pages, and lately had included such superstars as Michael Bolton, George Michael (both then CBS acts), and the woman perceived as Mariah's main competition, Whitney Houston.

None of this was in Mariah's career plan. What she wanted was for Ben Margulies and her to produce the album themselves. After all, they knew the material better than anyone. Given a good studio and a decent budget, rather than the cramped quarters and rudimentary equipment of Bedworks, they were sure they'd be able to achieve it. As Mariah put it, "I wasn't open to working with a superstar producer." It was a natural feeling. She and Ben had worked on this material for three years. Much of it had been written when Mariah was still in high school. They'd *created* it. The songs had come out of their ideas and improvisations. They'd taken the skeletons, the germs of tunes, and put flesh on the bones, working night after night, take after take, until they had what they considered a very good demo. And now, with the result of all those hours of labor so close to seeing fruition, the last stage was going to be taken away from them. As Ben resignedly told Fred Bronson, "It's inevitably what happens, and you hope that people handle [the songs] with care."

Once the names had been selected, meetings had to be arranged, and the producers introduced to Mariah and her voice. Tommy Mottola contacted them all personally—a measure of the importance he placed on this project. Narada Michael Walden promised to sit down with Mariah when he was in New York. When that time came, he found her to be "very shy" and a fan of George Michael (a sound choice, given that Walden had been his producer). Still, it offered a starting point for their working relationship.

When Rhett Lawrence received the call inviting him to New York, all he was told was that the singer was eighteen and possessed "the most incredible voice you've ever heard." On arriving and hearing her tape, he was forced to agree. "I literally got goose bumps on my arms when I heard her sing. I couldn't believe the power and maturity in her voice."

Ric Wake had a similar assessment when Mottola played him Mariah's demo tape. "It was obvious that she was great—she was amazing." Their meeting occurred on a Wednesday; Mottola asked if he could begin working with her the next day. As it happened, he could. Mariah appeared at his house, and things clicked between them. Their very first writing session produced "There's Got to Be a Way," which would end up on the album.

For all that Mariah aspired to produce herself, she happily and gratefully accepted the label's choices. As she later put it, "They did put me with different producers that they wanted to have me work with, and this being the first album, I took a certain amount of direction from the record company. You know, they are taking a chance." At the same time, she stated her goals for the future in no uncertain terms: "Ideally, though, I'd like to be involved with everything." Ric Wake, at least, was given a cassette containing demos of twelve songs that Mariah and Ben had penned together. For such a young, new pair, it was an impressive collection, and several of the tunes would end up, rerecorded, on the album. Musically, they were elaborate constructions, and as Ben said, "They were very close to what's on the album, if not almost exactly"—a tribute both to his ability and the amount of effort expended by the pair. Lyrically, Mariah tended to dwell on relationships. At least that was her metaphor. The songs weren't "necessarily" about them; she was merely putting the events of her own life into a context that everyone could relate to.

Signing that contract proved to be an inspiration for Mariah and Ben. Within a week of Mariah's putting her name on the dotted line, the ink barely dry, the two had written something new. Again, the lyrics seemed to be concerned with romance, but actually it was a celebration of their recent good fortune, a song called "Vision of Love." It found its way onto the CBS tape that circulated to the producers.

However, there was still more writing to be done, and for this the company paired Mariah with her producers. She approached it all gamely. With Walden and Wake, she worked in New York (although the recordings with Walden were done at Tarpan Studios in San Rafael, California). For Lawrence, Mariah traveled to Los angeles. It was there that he heard the demo for "Vision of Love" and realized its potential as a hit, but not as it currently stood—"a fifties sort of shuffle." Mariah needed a more contemporary sound than that. So Lawrence, Mariah, Ben, and Chris Toland worked together on the arrangement in the studio. The tempo was changed, session musicians were brought in to add guitars and bass (although Ben received credit for drums and programming on the final track), and Mariah recorded a new vocal. Her original vocal from the demo wasn't scrapped, though; it remained in the song as the second vocal in the chorus. Then, with some additional studio gloss, it was finished.

"There's Got to Be a Way" was the product of that first writing session between Mariah and Ric Wake. "[I]t went from there," he remembered later. "We did four songs together." However, "There's Got to Be a Way" was the only fruit of those joint compositions to make it onto the record produced by Wake and Walden.

"I Don't Wanna Cry" came about in the writing time Mariah and Narada Michael Walden spent together. They'd worked on several songs; then he decided to "slow the tempo down" and try to create one of "those 'crying' type of ballads" that descended in a direct line from gospel music and which he'd heard so often while growing up. Once the song was on tape, he had a firsthand chance to see the standards of perfection that Mariah imposed upon herself. Walden was perfectly happy with what they had; it was all in the can, and he believed Mariah was pleased with it, too. Then she called him. There was one line that, on repeated plays, troubled her. She'd had a better idea, and she wanted to change it—which she did, not once, but two or three times as Walden flew the tapes to her in New York. Not only did she fix the line, but she also had some more ideas, and added them. Finally,

Walden had to call her and say, "Look, I used your lick on that thing because you like it, but the other stuff you're adding on, you really don't need." It took him a little while to convince her. Even so, as an experienced producer, he remained gratified by her professional attitude. "Mariah was nineteen, twenty years old, making her first album. She really wanted it to be special."

(When asked to compare Mariah to his most recent superstar, Whitney Houston, Walden was very diplomatic: "Both are tremendous singers," he said, ". . . I'm honored to be able to work with both of them.")

"Someday" was another Carey-Margulies composition—as was the majority of the completed album—and a tune that caught Ric Wake's attention from the first time he played the tape Tommy Mottola had given him. "I loved that song right from the beginning. . . . Then Mariah called me one day and said, 'I'd love to do it if you want to do it.' It was great—I'm glad she called me."

It had been one of the four songs on the demo tape Mottola had plucked from Mariah's hand at the party, strong enough in its early form to impress the label president. Ben Margulies described that version as "very simple and funky. It had a simplicity to it that kind of drew you into it," and he approved of the finished product (of which he was co-arranger), calling it "really simple and clean," and adding, "The point came across."

Like so many of the pieces Mariah and Ben wrote, it began as an improvisation—in this case, over a bass-and-drum line—a dance groove in the New Jack Swing/hip-hop vein. While Ben tried out chord changes on the keyboard, Mariah would find vocal melody lines and choruses. Then, as Ben recorded the instrumental track, working with synthesizers, sequencers, drum machines, and computers, she'd be busy completing a set of lyrics.

But even with all the planning and expensive technology, happy accidents could—and did—happen in the studio. Mariah recounted one of these, which occurred while she was working with Ric Wake and Ben on the vocal for "All in Your Mind": "I was using my upper register . . . what happened was at the end of it, I did these vocal flips. When I was doing it, my voice split and went into a harmony. If you hear it, it splits. I was saying, 'Get rid of that,' but everyone said, 'No way, we're keeping that.' "

BEFORE THE RECORDING process was even complete, at Black Rock (the nickname for CBS Columbia's corporate headquarters in New York) meetings were being held and a plan formulated to ensure that the public would sit up and take a great deal of notice of Mariah Carey. The campaign to be mounted would be massive, the largest and most expensive the label had undertaken to "break" an artist since Bruce Springsteen was marketed to the United States in 1975 with his *Born to Run* album. And it was as closely organized as any military campaign.

Mariah had been given the designation of "priority artist"; in other words, making her a star was of paramount importance, and careers were on the line. As Jane Berk, former director of marketing for CBS Records, told the *New York Times,* "We had numerous, numerous meetings about Mariah way in advance of the album's release. It was about carefully planting seeds in the industry and nurturing their development at every stage. It was very strategically planned. We went out on a limb, and it was worth taking the risk." Producer Ric Wake, who observed the furor, concurred: "There was so much momentum, and everyone was pushing so hard from every level. There were so many decisions being made."

Of course, it didn't hurt that Mariah had as her mentor the new head of the label's domestic operations. When the boss speaks, everyone underneath is very likely to listen—and then jump as high as possible.

The marketing plan for Mariah was unusual. The way to do things, it was decided, was to put her before people with a great deal of influence, at the convention of the National Association of Recording Merchandisers (NARM) in Los Angeles in the spring of 1990. This would introduce her to the buyers for all the nation's large record chains, a powerful group that controlled the quantities ordered of each album and which was therefore in a position to push a new artist. Mariah's performance there was to be preceded by a specially produced video presentation detailing her life and the making of her record. It was a bold move, but one that, if it was successful, would reap some very handsome dividends.

"The energy level in that room was astounding," observed Howard Appelbaum, vice president and head buyer of the Kemp Mill chain in Maryland. But regarding Mariah's actual performance—where she was backed by the late Richard Tee on piano, and singers Patrique McMillan, Billy T. Scott, and Trey Lorenz— he was somewhat less enthusiastic, stating that she was "good, not incredible." But then, the pressure on Mariah was tremendous, and it was virtually her first public singing appearance. (Virtually, but not quite; a few weeks earlier, CBS had debuted her in an invitation-only soiree in New York—a boost for executives and senior sales representatives, the people who would be called upon to sell her talent. For that performance, Mariah was as close to solo as she would ever be, accompanied only by Tee.)

Following their game plan, Columbia capitalized on the exposure Mariah had gained at the NARM convention by sending her on a nine-city promotional mini-tour, which allowed both record-store and radio personnel to meet and hear her. The usual procedure for labels was to send out tapes and hope someone in a position of authority heard them. But in this case, no chances were being taken. As Jane Berk explained, "We wanted to make sure people listened to Mariah—so we sent her." A risky tactic, it seemed to work. After seeing her again, during her appearance in Philadelphia, Appelbaum increased his chain's order for her album. And, following Mariah's visit to San Francisco, that city's station began playing an advance copy of "Vision of Love," claiming to be the first in the country to do so. This was an extremely encouraging sign, as the station was thought of as a leader in the industry, which meant that others would soon be playing the song.

On the road, Mariah was accompanied by Patrique, Billy, and

Trey, a group who not only kept the atmosphere lighthearted, but helped make this new, tense experience bearable for Mariah. What was essentially a boring venture—touring—became fun for her as they cracked jokes, argued, and gossiped around her.

She'd met them in February during the sessions for the album, when she recorded "There's Got to Be a Way," which employed Billy T. Scott and his ensemble as part of the group of backing vocalists. (Billy also appeared on "All in Your Mind.") Trey was a friend of one of the vocalists and came to the studio. As Mariah recalled, "I heard someone singing all the high, top notes with me, and I'm like, 'Who is *that?*' I turned around and it was Trey." It was the beginning of a beautiful friendship.

NOW, WITH THE album complete, all ten tracks of it, and the promotional tour under way, Mariah should have been focusing on the present. But that wasn't her style. Although her first disc hadn't even reached the stores yet—the mastering was finished and it was being pressed—she was looking ahead to her next album. She and Ben had even written the first song for it, when she was back in New York for the weekend.

Traveling again, and surrounded by the upper echelon of label executives—Tommy Mottola, Don Ienner, Bobby Colomby—she played them the rough work tape she and Ben had put together of "Love Takes Time." It was plain, even crude, just piano and voice, but its impact was undeniable. The consensus was universal: "This is a number one record. You have to put this in that album." It wasn't exactly what Mariah wanted to hear. After too many grueling months in the studio, she was ready for a break.

But management was adamant. The song would be added to *Mariah Carey,* as the album had been titled. It was, quite literally, a case of stopping the presses. The demo was rushed to Walter Afanasieff, a studio whiz (he was responsible for the arrangements on the first three Whitney Houston albums). His work with Narada Michael Walden had so impressed Mottola and Ienner that they'd given him a job as an executive staff producer with Columbia. Afanasieff was astonished at the opportunity. After all, Mariah had been working with top names, and he was still a relative unknown—at that point, he'd never produced anything by himself. But time was of the essence, and he buckled down to the job. As it was, the rhythm and instrumental tracks were cut in one very long day. Then Walter stepped on a plane to New York and the Hit Factory studio where Mariah "did her vocals. She did all the backgrounds, practically sang all night. . . . We came back to the studio that afternoon, and we had to fix one line that we needed to get from Mariah."

As soon as that was done, it was back to the West Coast and to Sausalito's The Plant studios to mix the song into its final form. So, in a three-day marathon, from start to finish, "Love Takes Time" was done. Or that was what Walter thought. Columbia decided the vocals needed to be louder. Time was quickly running out on his big break, and he knew it. But, as the clock ticked down to the deadline, he finished.

Even then, the first copies of *Mariah Carey* didn't list the "Love Takes Time" track on the sleeve, although it was on the disc. "I don't know if they had to throw away a few hundred copies," Ben Margulies commented to Fred Bronson. But even if they had, Columbia thought it was worthwhile. They were certain the tune would be a smash.

OF COURSE, NO album could be launched without a video, and with Mariah tagged as a "priority artist," that was particularly true. "The visual element was a very, very, very important part of exposing this artist," was the way Jane Berk put it, and while she was also referring to print ads, there was little doubt that she primarily meant video. For Mariah was prime material: young, attractive, photogenic, with a trailing mass of honey-blond curls, and statuesque (standing five feet, nine inches tall). And networks like MTV and VH-1 had definitely been proven to have a huge impact on artists' careers—one only needed to look at Madonna to see that.

With "Vision of Love" selected as the first single, a video was ordered and shot. But the finished product failed to impress the Columbia top brass, and without any hesitation it was scrapped and another ordered. "The special treatment really upset me," a disgruntled former label employee said. "They spend $200,000 on a video and Mariah doesn't like it. No big deal." One source estimated the total cost of both videos at $450,000, a figure refuted by Ienner ("total bullshit"), although he did admit, "If we're gonna take the time and effort that we did with Mariah, on every level, then we're going to image her the right way. If it costs a few extra dollars to make a splash in terms of the right imaging, you go ahead and do it."

Luckily, the new clip, produced by Ron Kay, satisfied everyone. The last piece was in place.

JUNE 1990 WAS a very busy month for Mariah Carey, as the marketing machine at Columbia moved into top gear. In record stores all across the country, her face stared out from displays, singing into an old-fashioned microphone. In *Billboard,* the music-industry trade paper, a total of five full-page ads were bought for her upcoming album. And, in a completely unprecedented coup, Mariah was beamed into millions of homes, appearing before the first game of the 1990 NBA playoffs to sing "America the Beautiful," a spot almost invariably reserved for established stars. It indicated just how much muscle CBS was exerting—at Tommy Mottola's behest—on her behalf.

But the deluge of publicity didn't stop there; indeed, it was just beginning. As the *Vision of Love* video began airing in heavy rotation on MTV, Mariah was on national television again—not just once, but twice, guesting on both "The Arsenio Hall Show" and "The Tonight Show." All the stops were pulled out for this one. As a rather bewildered Mariah said, almost apologetically, "I didn't get the chance to work my way up from clubs. All of a sudden, I was on 'Arsenio Hall.' It's scary."

She didn't really need to worry. Columbia had done everything in its considerable power to ensure her success, and on June 2, when "Vision of Love" entered the *Billboard* Hot 100 at number 73, followed on June 30 by *Mariah Carey* debuting on the Album 200 at number 80, it seemed Columbia had done its job quite effectively. Exactly *how* effectively was only discovered a few weeks later.

Both the single and the album continued to climb the charts. On August 4, 1990, "Vision of Love" reached its peak at number 1 on the *Billboard* Hot 100, where it stayed for four weeks. Then its parent record hit the top of the album charts, beginning a remarkable run of twenty-two consecutive weeks in that position. (In the U.K., *Mariah Carey* would debut at its highest position, number 6.) Mariah dedicated the album to her sister Alison (by this time a housewife, still living on Long Island), but also took great care in the acknowledgments to thank everybody who'd helped her along the way—from Patricia to the Columbia staff to the creator of her gift, God. Never selfish with her gratitude, she didn't want anyone to be overlooked.

Mariah Carey had made her splash. And it was a very, very big one.

AS MARIAH HAS pointed out, "I make pop music," and that's exactly what *Mariah Carey* was. From ballads to dance beats, it traversed the spectrum of popular music, infusing it all with an overtone of the gospel, soul, and R&B sounds she loved.

"Vision of Love," the leadoff track, was the perfect introduction to her voice. With an ideal slow-dancing tempo, it still managed to swing, with Mariah's backing vocals (herself multitracked) answering her lead. On the final chorus, her voice flew toward those trademark high notes before the instruments dropped out, leaving Mariah to sing her way to the tune's climax alone.

"There's Got to Be a Way" was, lyrically, a piece of social concern about some of the ills in our society: homelessness, apartheid, bigotry (a subject close to Mariah's heart), and famine. Restrained in the verses, the chorus had a "churchy" feel, mostly due to the backing vocals, which began to take off before the middle instrumental break and then soared at the key change close to the song's end as Mariah began to demonstrate fully the extent of her range, flitting through the upper register like a bird.

The ballad "I Don't Wanna Cry"—reminiscent in both rhythm and arrangement of Wham!'s "Careless Whispers"—opened with an attractive acoustic guitar line and then featured the powerful lower end of Mariah's range, one which had exactly the right dramatic power for such an emotional song, with its clever pause beat as emphasis before the last chorus. Equally soothing and draining, it served notice of the timeless quality of 's voice.

"Someday," four tracks into the disc, was the first dance song; given the reputation that Mariah had acquired as a dance artist (or "dance droid" as one critic disparagingly put it), that might have been a surprise. But her performance was more than credible, even if the song didn't offer her the challenge of the slower material. Over a bouncy, highly percussive beat, the melody bubbled, going into a soft, double-tracked rap before fading out over a chorus and Mariah's piercing high note.

"Vanishing" stood in complete contrast, utterly stark, just piano and Mariah's voice. She was able to produce the track herself—as she'd hoped to do for the whole album—and its intimacy stood in counterpoint to what she saw as "too much production" on the rest of the record. The gospel influence was particularly evident here, with the rougher feel of the keyboard, and a multi-tracked choir of Mariahs' offering background vocals. While many critics just ignored the tune in their reviews, Alan Jackson of the prestigious *London Observer* deemed it *the* "outstanding track," and indeed, its very sparseness added considerably to its simple power.

"All in Your Mind" was another ballad, one based around a strong, memorable chorus, which briefly showcased the extreme high end of Mariah's vocal reach. (Probably not since the late Min-nie Ripperton had anyone managed to reach so high a note on a record.) Built around some basic keyboard arpeggios—played here by Ben Margulies—the two short verses merely acted as bridges between choruses, the song's real muscle.

It led into "Alone in Love," a Rhett Lawrence–produced ballad. Other than the synthesized instrumentation, this seemed, like the previous track, almost out of place on a nineties record, having far more the feel of a timeless standard. That could actually be said for much of *Mariah Carey;* the basis of its music was not in contemporary fads and fashions, but rather the material looked backward for its inspiration, to soul, some jazz, and especially gospel. In that regard, its success definitely bucked the trend, and sent a hopeful song for the future.

A guest slot by Living Color's guitarist Vernon Reid, blasting an Eddie Van Halen–style solo, opened "You Need Me," a dance track that gained its impact through a poppish chorus, studio effects on the vocals, and a powerful, concise, middle guitar break.

"Sent from Up Above" slowed the tempo slightly, with an arrangement that owed a great deal to seventies soul, particularly softer bands like those of the Chi-Lites, but with some nineties technological touches to brighten its appeal.

The penultimate track, "Prisoner," was utterly contemporary, the most upbeat piece on the album. Opening with a low rap, it kept a vibrant dance bpm (beats per minute) throughout, more or less pulling the words and melody along to the rhythm.

And then, finally, there was the song that had stopped the presses: "Love Takes Time," another Carey-Margulies ballad, with a chorus that slipped into the brain and wouldn't go away. It fitted very well into the overall context of *Mariah Carey,* both musically and thematically, and certainly presented a stronger finish to the disc than "Prisoner" would have done.

Whether the album would have ended up doing as well without the label's gigantic marketing push remains one of those questions that can never be answered. It used the best talents available, both in producers and session musicians, and the arrangements achieved exactly what was intended, serving as a backdrop for Mariah's voice, which was (as it should have been) the record's focal point. While all the songs were strong, it was the ballads that better suited Mariah at this stage and brought out her personality, something Columbia obviously realized, because slower songs comprised the majority of the disc. The dance music, as so often happened in that genre, tended to submerge her in the beat.

But perhaps the greatest strength of *Mariah Carey* was that it didn't target any one specific audience. There was enough variety on it to appeal to almost everyone. That it did just that was evident when the single "Vision of Love" and the album topped not only the pop charts, but also the R&B and Adult Contemporary charts, fully vindicating Tommy Mottola's judgment in signing her to the label and causing him to say, "Mariah is one of the greatest singers ever."

The reviewers were quick to pick up on Mariah's astonishing range as the album's selling point—"all seven octaves of it," as David Gates wrote in *Newsweek,* "from purring alto to stratospheric shriek. Up in this dog-whistle register, she can shape a scream into precise, synthesizer-like phrases." He did note, however, "She has the good taste not to overuse this device, but how could anyone—especially a twenty-year-old—resist showing off just a little?"

New York Newsday took a similar tack: "Young pop singers with such extensive ranges often sacrifice emotion for technique, and there are times on Carey's debut album . . . when that's the case. She'll accelerate into upper-register notes that sound like high-pitched whistles. . . . But for the most part Carey keeps her technique in check and uses her voice in service of the song." Hillel Italie waxed rhapsodic about Mariah's vocal agility: "This is a voice that can probably shatter glass and put it back together, that sounds as if she's taking the words and twirling them over her head like a cowboy with a lasso." And an enthusiastic review in *People* cited her "extraordinary control, driving power, lovely pitch, and wide range," and added that she "has one of those voices that could probably be entertaining singing the phone book."

However, the praise wasn't completely unreserved. *Newsweek's* Gates wasn't impressed by the songs, which ranged, he thought, "from banal love complaints to a banal save-the-world anthem." This was echoed by *People,* where Ralph Novak believed that "she would have profited from outside help," and the album, "striking as it is, could have been spectacular with better raw material."

From the sales figures, though, the public obviously had no complaints about the raw material. *Mariah Carey* quickly went platinum (one million copies sold) and would eventually go on to sell more than 6 million copies. In fact, this debut by Columbia's pop diva outsold *I'm Your Baby Tonight* by Arista's darling, Whitney Houston, by more than 2 million copies, a clear indication that Mariah was stealing away some of her fans.

It wasn't only the album that continued to sell. When "Vision of Love" vanished from the charts, "Love Takes Time" was there to take its place, spending two weeks at number 1 (coincidentally, both songs entered the Hot 100 at number 73). Following that, it was the turn of "Someday," which lasted at the top spot for another two weeks, beginning on March 9, 1991; then "I Don't Wanna Cry," which was there for yet another two weeks. The run of hit singles was just as remarkable as the album sales; it made Mariah the first act since the Jackson Five to have her first four singles top the charts, something not achieved by Whitney Houston or any of the other pop divas who had preceded her.

THE IDEA OF performing scared Mariah. She'd made no secret of the fact that she was essentially introverted. "I'm not into performing," she told Stephen Holden in *The New York Times.* "I have to make myself do it because it comes with the territory." But as the album and the singles rose through the charts, there was actually only one live commitment, made earlier, that she had to fulfill. The

KMEL Summer Jam, held at Shoreline Amphitheater in Mountain View, California, was probably the single largest R&B/soul event of the year.

More than ten acts comprised the bill on August 5, 1990, the day after "Vision of Love" hit number 1. They included Tony!Toni!Toné!, Johnny Gill, and Bell Biv Devoe, all certainly quite famous in their own right. The headliner was MC Hammer, whose "U Can't Touch This" had been a monster hit (although he would quickly disappear from sight, attempting to return in 1994 in full fake gangsta fashion). For Mariah, whose experience with live work had been limited to small showcases or television, it must have been daunting to suddenly find herself having to perform in front of thousands of people—and as a support act, at that! By all accounts, she acquitted herself well, overcoming whatever nervousness she felt to deliver a short but powerful set that, naturally, included a well-received rendition of the nation's biggest song. But notably, except for taping MTV's "Unplugged" program and "Showtime at the Apollo," she wouldn't perform again in front of an audience for more than three years.

ALONG WITH MARIAH'S gigantic success came the photographers and reporters. Everyone suddenly wanted to write a feature or take a picture or have a piece of her. She was hot. But unlike so many who view success as a license to go wild, Mariah continued her quiet, low-key approach to life. No social whirl, no nightclubbing, no evenings of photo opportunities for the paparazzi. Her biggest indulgence was a new car—a Mustang convertible—and a new place to live, where she didn't have to sleep on the floor or share space with roommates.

She didn't move that far—just to New York's Upper East Side, where she found a one-bedroom apartment with a stunning view on the twenty-first floor of a high-rise building, a place to live with her two Persian cats, Ninja (all black) and Thompkins (all white), and which she could decorate with her Marilyn Monroe posters. Monroe, another star who'd experienced a poor child-hood and whose career as the nation's sex symbol ended tragically in the early sixties with her suicide, had long been a fascination of Mariah's. A friend disclosed, "Aside from the negative aspects of her life, she sort of idolized her. She liked the overall concept of being famous and the way Marilyn Monroe came to fame."

And Mariah was certainly famous enough herself these days; she had become the star she'd once told her high-school teachers and guidance counselor that she'd be. As her best friend Patricia Johnson said, Mariah "always did what she said she was going to do."

Not that fame offered Mariah any greater opportunity to relax. "Vision of Love" had a video, and each new single demanded an-other, which represented hours of work and even more hours of boredom. For "Love Takes Time," she spent "most of the time preparing for the video in the trailer," as rain kept interrupting the shoot.

The final, acceptable clip for "Vision of Love" kept Mariah on a fairly stark stage set, before a backdrop of speeding clouds, an eerily lit sky, and a single tree with a swing. The overall simplic-ity of the design focused attention where it belonged—on Mariah and on the song. It *worked*. In all likelihood, we will never know what the scrapped video looked like, but this made it all irrelevant. In terms of presenting a new artist, it was perfect, unpretentious, evocative of solitude, loneliness, and, somehow, hope.

"Love Takes Time" was even more romantic, shot in soft-focus black and white on a beach. Translating a song to a video concept was an arduous task, but Walter Maser did a splendid job. The empty phone booth, with its receiver dangling and twirling, stood as a particularly powerful image of lost love, and a heartbroken Mariah, wandering along the sand, in and out of the surf, only ac-centuated that idea.

"I Don't Wanna Cry" again found Mariah as the sole face on the screen, bathed in red and orange lights as she walked around a stage. Behind her, instruments and microphones were set up, as if for a performance, once more highlighting the loneliness of the ballad's lyrics.

As befitted its outgoing, upbeat tempo, "Someday" featured a more substantial cast. Mariah herself took a hand in the planning of this video, which was shot at a high school in Bayonne, New Jersey. She'd come up with the original concept of a young girl (based on herself) and a young boy, and then collaborated with director Larry Jordan, adding more ideas until they had a completed storyboard. Working and being able to interact with others, particularly a group of six- to twelve-year-olds, was "the most fun" she'd experienced in making a video. It was also gratifying for her to be able to include Larry Wright, a "great" street drummer who had come to her attention via a PBS documentary. Prominently featured among the kids was a hyperactive six-year-old hip-hop dancer who stole the spotlight whenever he was on camera.

The collected videos soon found commercial release as *Mariah Carey: The First Vision,* and promptly entered both the U.S. and U.K. video charts. Featuring the clips for "Vision of Love," "Love Takes Time," "I Don't Wanna Cry," and an extended version of "Someday," the set also contained an insightful interview with Mariah, offering some more details of her childhood and pre-stardom experiences. In addition, it included footage shot during rehearsals for her "Saturday Night Live" spot on October 27, 1990 (where a happy Mariah clowned and warmed up with Billy, Patrique, and Trey), and during preparations for her performance on "Showtime at the Apollo." Playing at Harlem's Apollo Theater, which had at one time or another hosted all her soul-music idols, was a huge thrill for Mariah.

All of this helped to make the video special, but the highlight perhaps was the two songs filmed at an early showcase gig at New York's Club Tatou. Accompanied by a small group (piano, keyboards, bass, drums, and Billy, Trey, and Patrique on backing vocals), Mariah sang "Vanishing" and "Don't Play That Song," a soul tune made famous "by the incomparable Aretha Franklin." Franklin's influence on Mariah was obvious in the phrasing and dynamics of the piece, and in the gospel manner in which she carried syllables across the line breaks and improvised upon the written melody lines.

ALL THE TRIUMPHS of 1990 were marvelous, and at year's end came the crowning jewels, as Mariah found herself nominated for an astonishing five Grammys: Best Pop Vocal Performance, Female, for "Vision of Love"; Best New Artist; Album of the Year; Song of the Year (again for "Vision of Love"); and Best Album. This made her only the third person in the entire history of the Grammy Awards to be nominated for Best New Artist, Best Album, and Song of the Year all at the same time. Pretty good for a rookie.

The 33rd Annual Grammy Awards were held at New York's Radio City Music Hall on February 20, 1990. The show was broadcast to sixty countries. Wearing a short, tight black dress trimmed in silver, Mariah awaited the announcements of the winners in her categories, and also prepared for her own performance. She later appeared onstage to sing "Vision of Love" for an audience that would total many millions around the globe (this performance would later be available as part of the *Great Moments of the Grammys* CD collection).

As the evening wore on, and the count of winners and losers grew, Mariah made two more trips to the stage, where she collected Grammys for Best New Artist and Best Pop Vocal Performance, Female. The sheer delight on her face in the photographs taken afterward said it all. Not only had she been accepted by the public, she'd also been heartily embraced by the music establishment, joining a small, elite group of multiple-Grammy winners.

That alone could have been the icing on the cake. But within a month, Mariah's mantelpiece must have been crowded with trophies. The *Rolling Stone* Readers' Pick Music Awards named her Best New Female Singer. Then, on March 12, at the Fifth Annual "Soul Train" Awards, held at the Shrine Auditorium in Los Angeles, Mariah walked away with three more awards: Best New

R&B/Urban Contemporary Artist; Best R&B/Urban Contemporary Single, Female; and Best R&B/Urban Contemporary Album. It was as sure a sign as any that the African American community had accepted her music. Then, just to round things off, Mariah and Ben took Song of the Year honors for "Love Takes Time" at the BMI 40th Annual Pop Awards dinner, held on May 19 at the Regent Beverly Wilshire Hotel in Los Angeles, with additional honors given for both "Vision of Love" and "Someday," while "I Don't Wanna Cry" received a citation. The effect of all these awards—most especially the Grammys—was to increase the reorders from stores for Mariah's album. With her name before the public again (as if it hadn't been there enough in the last few months!), there was an increased demand for her music.

HOWEVER, THE FULL measure of fame is never complete until the backlash comes around. The press, it seems, delights in creating heroes and idols, only to promptly tear them down again as the full "truth" comes out.

In Mariah's case, the backlash began early, almost before she'd had the luxury of resting on the laurels of her success. First, there was little more than rumor and innuendo—she and Tommy Mottola were supposedly romantically involved. In mid-1990, Mottola and his wife of nineteen years, Lisa Clark Mottola, had signed a separation agreement, which allowed him generous visitation rights to their two children. But he was adamant in denying all reports that linked him to Mariah in anything other than business. Still, some said, there had to be an ulterior motive for all the attention he'd lavished on her career and the push Columbia had given her album . . . there could be no smoke without fire.

As for Mariah, she really didn't want to talk about it. "There is not much that is sacred in this business," she said. "But to me, my private life is." When questioned, she did admit to having a boyfriend, but she was unwilling to offer any details.

The other accusation leveled at her was far more serious. It was bandied around that Mariah was trying to exploit the black community by being yet another white singer attempting to sound black; she was a rip-off. This demanded immediate action, and interviews were quickly set up with two leading black publications, *Jet* and *Ebony*.

Such an attack must have been felt by Mariah on a very deep and personal level. After all, the scars of racial intolerance weren't that old. She'd seen it contribute to the breakup of her parents' marriage, and she knew the misery it had caused both her brother and sister when they were growing up. And, while Mariah had never hidden her background, neither was it something she'd chosen to make an issue of. Why should it even have been necessary? Couldn't people just accept her as she was—a person, Mariah Carey, the girl from Long Island? But, she explained, "Some people look at me and they see my light skin and my hair. I can't help the way I look, because it's me. I don't try to look a certain way or sing a certain way. I'm just trying to be me. And if people enjoy my music, then they shouldn't care what I am, so it shouldn't be an issue." And as she told *Ebony,* "If you look a certain way everybody goes, 'White girl,' and I'd go, 'No, that's not what I am.' "

The articles seemed to defuse the issue before it really took hold. But it must, at some level, have cast a minor pall on the year for her. All her life she'd had to cope with prejudice. Now, even with fame, she couldn't escape it entirely.

All in all, though, it had been an amazing beginning. For her, "the thrills [had] come in stages," which had moved very rapidly—seeing her album in the store, appearing on television, hearing her songs on the radio, being number 1 in *Billboard!* Why, exactly, had she struck such a deep, resonant chord in people? Yes, the marketing had helped tremendously, both in distributing her product and getting her name known, but the bottom line was that if people didn't like her music, they wouldn't buy it, no matter how it was packaged. The annals of the music business are littered with names that were hyped for a while, only to fall by the wayside and become footnotes because, in the end, nobody bought their records.

Mariah was giving people what they wanted. She had a large amount of talent. That surely helped, but other talented performers had failed to connect. She'd been lucky, and that was virtually a necessity for success. She was young enough for a large segment of the record-buying audience to easily relate to her—when she collected those two Grammys she was still only twenty. And she had dedication, an unwavering faith in her own ability. Yes, maybe she'd only really struggled for a year, "the lean year," she'd laughingly call it later, but during that time she'd used almost every spare moment in service of her career.

In all probability, the reason for her success was a combination of all those factors, mixed with her freshness. That she'd cowritten all her material was particularly important. After all, it's easier to invest your own words with emotion than someone else's, and people can tell, at some instinctive level, if that ache in your voice is real or faked. And her commitment set her far apart from the other pop divas on the scene. She did not become just another singer who arrived at the studio, punched in her vocals, went home, and then collected her royalty checks. She had a great deal invested in every note. With every song, she was putting herself on the line, showing her heart, exposing her sadness, or offering inspiration to others—a positive message, which, from a figure in the spotlight, can often do a vast amount of good.

What mattered, ultimately, was that she *had* succeeded. But while some people in the same position might have found their heads turned, Mariah was fine, her feet planted very firmly on the ground, thanks in large part to her mother, who'd filled her with very strong values, both social and artistic, and always bolstered her belief in herself. Mariah may have been proud of her album "for a first effort," but like any true artist, she was "never satisfied with her work"; there was always something she could have improved or done differently. But, in the brief moment when she was able to rest her feet in one of her many new pairs of shoes (or sneakers) or change into a new outfit, the evidence of her perspective on 1990 was best summed up when she smiled and said, "It beats waitressing, right?"

It most certainly did. And this was only the beginning.

4

T he question was, where did Mariah go from here? A number 1 album, four number 1 singles. How could she ever hope to top that? What should her next move be? Indeed, what was left to conquer? For most acts, the logical next step would be a massive tour, if not throughout the world, then at least a long string of dates in the United States, in arenas and large halls, and then a few selected shows in England and Japan. It would consolidate the fan base that had been established and give the crowds a chance to see their idol in the flesh.

But Mariah, as she had said, was not inclined toward live performance. At least, not yet. She knew it was something she'd have to undertake eventually. She liked the idea of traveling, but not the endless nights in hotel rooms. They affected her main asset, her voice, and that alone was a perfectly good reason to put off performing. Without her voice, she couldn't give a good show, and if she was going to do one, she was going to do it right. "I need a lot of sleep," she said, "and my songs are all strenuous." She had a very accurate gauge of her abilities and, more importantly, her limitations.

Nor was she particularly comfortable with the amount of attention she'd been receiving since her rise to stardom. "I don't want to be about hype and media," Mariah explained, showing just how modest and self-effacing she was at heart. "I don't want to put myself in everyone's face and make them sick of me." That had happened before, to too many artists whose spell in the sun then proved all too brief. Mariah Carey was developing a *career* in music. She intended to be around for a long time, doing exactly what she loved—if not always singing, then songwriting. And with 7 million copies of her first album sold, there was no danger that she'd ever have to return to waitressing or sweeping up hair.

Mariah's solution to the dilemma of what her next move would be was to begin working on her next album. "Well," she said, "I started writing for my second album immediately after I put out my first single from the first album, so I really didn't have a break. And it wasn't like, 'Oh, I have to follow up the success,' because it was just as the first single was taking off. Who knew what was going to happen to it, anyway? I didn't take a break because I just constantly write, and it was . . . a pattern that I established and I continue to do it."

Writing and recording also helped relieve some of the pressure that fame brought. "I started to record my second LP the moment I finished the first. I was so busy with that work that, at the beginning, I almost didn't know what was happening to me. Thank God, money didn't impress me and fame and success neither."

But for Mariah to even consider a new album at this stage was highly unusual. Within the music industry, it was accepted wisdom to wait at least two years between records, letting each play out its sales potential before releasing a new one—which would pick up new fans, who'd then find their way to the earlier catalogue. This way, sales of each disc could be maximized without the market seeming to be saturated by an artist's product.

In the sixties, things had been very different. Back then, groups and singers usually put out two albums a year, generally "driven," or highlighted, by a couple of hit singles that would be included, with the rest of the material, largely filler. The Beatles had altered that way of thinking. Writing their own songs (and being virtually the first artists to do so consistently) meant that every track on the album was strong, thus generating a demand for the long-playing record (LP) on its own merits. By the end of the decade, with the advent of album-oriented rock (AOR), the album slowly became far more important for sales than the single, eventually achieving dominance. Over the course of the next two decades, the marketing process for the album had become more and more sophisticated and refined. So what was Mariah's reason for being so different?

Columbia's decision to release a new Mariah Carey album "soon" was, they said, due to Mariah "growing so much from the last album." It was a perfectly believable situation for a singer and songwriter who was so young (just twenty-one!) and relatively new to the business. After all, Mariah must have learned a great deal during the year she'd spent in studios recording *Mariah Carey,* and even more in the time she'd spent promoting it.

THERE WAS, HOWEVER, something which appeared to stand as a large stumbling block: Mariah and Ben Margulies were no longer a writing partnership. A breach had occurred between them, which would prove irreparable. The reason, reportedly, was that long before Mariah inked her deal with Columbia, she had signed a contract with Ben. It entitled him to almost half of the money she earned from the album, as opposed to just half the royalties from the music-publishing rights of the songs they'd composed, to which he was, legally and morally, certainly entitled.

Looking back on the situation sometime later, Mariah said sadly, "I blindly signed. Later, I tried to make it right so we could continue . . . but he wouldn't accept it." For his part, Ben placed the blame on the music business, and expressed the hope of "getting back together in the not-too-distant future. . . . Hopefully, art will prevail over business."

And that was the way five years of friendship, of struggle and tough times, and of eventual triumph over adversity, ended.

One must wonder, though, what part—if any—the label played in all this. Is it possible that they'd paid heed to those reviewers who complained about the quality of the songs on *Mariah Carey?* Mariah and Ben had cowritten seven of those eleven songs. Granted, three of them had been smash hits, but Mariah was growing. Maybe it would be to her advantage to work with other people, to expand her horizons. She'd already proved she could do it—and very successfully.

COLUMBIA HAD ALREADY indicated that it was willing to give Mariah some latitude, both in material and production. "She deserves it," Don Ienner said. "She has a great feeling of what's right and what's wrong." And Tommy Mottola had already predicted, "I'm sure she wants to do a lot more on her next album, make it more stark."

She was already teaming up with a number of writers. There was the duo of David Cole and Robert Clivilles, whose ability to write and produce strong up-tempo material, was evidenced by a number of gold records and positive reviews from respected critics. (Of C + C Music Factory fame, Cole and Clivilles's "Gonna Make You Sweat" had been a huge hit, both on the charts and in the dance clubs.) And surprisingly, there was Walter Afanasieff, the man who'd produced "Love Takes Time" in such a rush. A Brazilian who'd immigrated to this country, he seemed an odd choice, as he had no track record of writing hit songs. But Mariah obviously felt relaxed and creative in his presence, and this was going to be her call—at least, within reason.

And then there was Carole King. She was a graduate of the Brill Building Music factory of the early sixties, where, with partner Gerry Goffin, she'd churned out a series of pop hits like "Up on the Roof" and "Will You Still Love Me Tomorrow?" But then she'd walked away from that to become a remarkably popular singer/songwriter. Her 1971 *Tapestry* album sold over 13 million copies and stayed on the charts for an unbelievable 302 weeks.

Perhaps surprisingly, it was King who first approached Mariah to ask if she'd be interested in recording a version of the Goffin-King song, "Natural Woman," which had been a big hit for Aretha Franklin. Mariah turned down the idea. Aretha, of course, was one of her idols, and since her recorded performance was already "untouchable," she felt there was nothing new she could bring to it. So, instead, Carole King left her home in Idaho to fly to New

York for one day and have a writing session with this young singer.

What came out of it was a ballad entitled "If It's Over," which Mariah described as "a true collaboration." The two sat and traded musical ideas, and Mariah came up with a set of lyrics, with work continuing until they had what they both described as "a wonderful song." And King added, "I love her voice. She's very expressive. She gives a lot of meaning to what she sings." This was praise and acceptance, not just from a contemporary, but from a veteran who'd literally heard thousands of other voices singing her songs.

That type of collaboration—sitting down, bouncing ideas off the other person—seemed to be Mariah's favorite way of working. She'd done it with Ben for several years. It worked with Carole King, and it seemed to work with Walter Afanasieff. In him, Mariah appeared to find a substitute for Ben, someone who was so eager to write with her that he would use every spare scrap of time for the venture.

For Mariah and Walter, the writing process had begun in late 1990, many months before any recording. Walter was involved in his latest project, spending long hours in the studio producing Michael Bolton's newest album. But when breaks would occur—such as when Bolton went off to play a few shows or take a short vacation—Walter took advantage of the opportunity to sit down and write with Mariah.

The creative sparks flew between them. He'd begin with an idea, something played on the keyboard, either a chord progression or a short instrumental line. In turn, this would inspire Mariah with ideas for a vocal melody or some lines of lyrics. Then, Walter said, as she would sing, "I start playing to what she's singing." And things would continue until the piece was finished and Mariah was satisfied with the words she'd penned.

It was eerily similar to the way Mariah and Ben had worked. Perhaps the main difference was that Walter's keyboard ability and knowledge of music theory were much greater than Ben's.

He could translate Mariah's vocal sketches into reality at much greater speed, with less guesswork.

"I always do the melody first," Mariah explained. "Sometimes I'll have an idea for a lyric. If I'm collaborating with someone, I'll direct them in the direction I'm going chordwise, because I get all these melody ideas and then I lose them if I don't have someone really good on keyboards right there with me. That's why I tend to collaborate because I lose the ideas by the time I figure out the chords. All these melody ideas just go."

It had originally been Tommy Mottola's idea to bring in David Cole and Robert Clivilles. It was a given that the new album would repeat the successful formula of mixing ballads and dance music, and who better for the dance music than the hottest team in the country?

As an established team, Clivilles and Cole already had their set way of working. They came to the writing session armed with plenty of ideas—"grooves," as they called them—and played them for Mariah, seeing which ones might work as the bases for songs. One decision they'd made right at the beginning was that they didn't want to emphasize Mariah's "high stuff." Although they knew it would be impossible to ignore it, they were both eager to steer clear of any criticism of trading on a gimmick. Instead, they planned to concentrate on bringing out Mariah's singing ability.

Mariah herself came to this second album with a few definite ideas. As Mottola had forecast, she wanted the sound to be more sparse, letting more space into the songs and allowing them to breathe. She was also quite determined to fight for her ideas, having given in to others' opinions too easily on *Mariah Carey*. ("I thought, 'Maybe they're right. They're big and famous and I'm just a new up-and-coming hopeful.'") And she was also keen for the overall sound to have a greater Motown and gospel influence—to reflect the sounds her brother and sister had played when she was very young, the music she'd gone on to discover herself. The gospel ideas had been there on the first album, but she wanted them deeper and stronger now.

More important than anything, though, was that she'd have what she'd lacked before; total involvement in the whole process, from writing to arranging to performing to producing. She'd be there every step of the way, more than happy to take responsibility for her own music.

By the start of spring 1991, Mariah had a large collection of songs at the demo stage, which she and Walter then played for the executives at Columbia, so they could decide which ones should be given the real treatment. The new album, once again, would be slightly weighted toward ballads. It had worked last time, was the thinking, and the emphasis here was to be on refinement, not innovation. Commercially, the ballads seemed to be Mariah's forte, and they gave her a chance to really sing, be it in her lower register or unleashing those angelic high notes. They'd also generated the most interest in the press, which was a factor worthy of consideration. But any style Mariah attempted she seemed to master with both ease and grace. It increased her musical options.

So, armed with a list of tunes which the label had approved (there was never a shadow of doubt about the inclusion of the Carey-King collaboration), Mariah once again found herself boarding planes and shuttling from coast to coast in pursuit of her art. Cole and Clivilles would produce the dance tracks with Mariah, and the other material would be a joint effort between Mariah and Walter.

The good weather was just beginning as she went into the studio. Unfortunately, she wouldn't see too much sunshine, keeping her usual night-owl hours, working from early evening until dawn, then sleeping the day away. It was, she said later, "like living in a cave." And recording studios certainly can be that way—isolated, insulated rooms away from the real world, without windows, artificially lit. Each might have its own character, but there remains a sameness that covers them all: Skywalker Sound in Marin County, The Plant in Sausalito, or Skyline, Axis, or Right Track in New York.

Working on this album was definitely a full-time job for

Mariah. Composing, singing, and producing weren't enough for her; she was also involved in arranging the tracks and singing most of the background vocals (something she'd done on the first album, and a process that seemed to hold an odd fascination for her). But, as she'd admitted, she loved being in the studio, most particularly singing there, building up layers of her voice and playing them back, carrying on until she'd achieved exactly what she was searching for.

While she might still not have thought of herself "as a big deal," as she put it, that wasn't the opinion of many others. Quite naturally, Columbia was eager for her new disc to repeat the success of *Mariah Carey,* and her fans were anxious to hear more of her voice. Could she deliver the goods again? And could these new partnerships produce strong enough songs?

THE ANSWERS TO those questions came—at least in part—when the first single from Mariah's new album was released and jumped into the *Billboard* Hot 100 on August 31, 1991, at number 35, the highest entry position of any of her singles to date. It was a bouncy dance tune—"Emotions," one of the four Carey-Cole-Clivilles collaborations—and also the album's title track. (Oddly, though, it wasn't originally planned as the first single; that was going to be "You're So Cold," the first song the trio completed together, which did end up on the record.)

The song's inspiration actually came from a group called the Emotions, who had scored their own number 1 hit in 1977 with "Best of My Love," a disco tune produced by Earth, Wind and Fire's Maurice White. Thoroughly likable, it didn't depend on any bass line or drum pattern, just a floating groove and a very memorable melody, and these were the qualities Mariah sought to emulate. "It definitely has the feeling from the Emotions," David Cole admitted, adding that it was Mariah who came up with the idea of using that band's name for the album title. "[W]e all decided, 'No, why not?' . . . It's a great name for a song."

Six weeks later, on October 12, after the album had been released, "Emotions" was number 1, where it remained for three weeks. That gave Mariah a unique piece of chart history. She was the first artist ever to have her first five singles all reach number 1, beating the Jackson Five's record of four, established twenty-one years earlier. It was a landmark achievement, and a very positive sign for the new album.

The single "Emotions" was followed by "Can't Let Go," which rapidly followed it onto the Hot 100. Unfortunately, it didn't quite manage to continue Mariah's amazing run of number 1 hits, peaking at a breath-catching number 2 as its predecessor, now a gold record, slipped down the Top Fifty.

"Make It Happen" was the third and final single from the album. With its catchy chorus, inspiring message, and bouncy beat, it seemed like a natural, rising up the chart through March of 1992. However, it stalled at number 5, the lowest place to date for any of Mariah's singles. (Almost everything she's released has made at least the Top Five, a claim that virtually no artist of today—or any other era—can make.)

BY HER OWN standards, the album succeeded. *"Emotions* has a little bit of an older-type vibe, a Motown feel," she told *New York* magazine. It displayed the increased confidence that two years had brought to Mariah, both in her vocal style and her lyrics.

The critics approached the album more cautiously than they had the first one, giving it more consideration, which, at the same time, meant viewing it more closely. Mariah had gone beyond the stage of being label hype to become an artist, and she was about to be treated like one.

David Hiltbrand, writing in *People,* said, "The material here is stronger and the arrangements richer," even if "as on her debut, the song selection is somewhat uneven." However, he was willing to acknowledge "that Carey is truly a transcendent talent." Christian Wright, in *New York Newsday,* found that, at least on one cut, "she infuses a torchy and breathy croon with the sort of genuine passion that was completely missing from the first album," and noted that *"Emotions* uses simpler arrangements so that the voice is showcased as the most important instrument."

From those words, it might be assumed that the reviewers thought that Mariah had more than adequately conquered the notorious sophomore jinx. However, they were still able to find plenty of faults. The most common one was that Mariah overused her now-famous upper register (which was odd, since she was actually quite sparing with it). The other was that she approached "everything at maximum intensity, even ballads." As Arion Berger stated in *Entertainment Weekly,* she "reaches for epiphany on every cut," although he was good enough to concede that the album "ticks along like a Swiss watch—finely tuned, glossily assembled, filled with precision instrumentals and spectacular vocal turns." But he had nothing good to say about Mariah's lyrics, calling them "hackneyed high school poetry" that "for most of the album . . . either lament[s] the recent departure of some cad or praise[s] the next Mr. Right." For "The Wind," the album's last track, *Newsday*'s Christian Wright took a completely different view, feeling that "Carey has written moving lyrics."

All of this largely went to prove there were as many opinions as there were writers. The real judging would come from the record buyers, people who were willing to shell out hard-earned money for an album.

In all likelihood, no one expected *Emotions* to sell in the same vast quantities as *Mariah Carey* had, let alone exceed it. Too little time had passed since Mariah's debut. She was, if anything, too much in the public eye. Mariah herself wasn't worried; she had her sense of security now. "If I wanted to stay home and write songs and make a moderate living, I could do that." It was the artistic satisfaction, not the commercial success, that was driving her.

In the final count, the sales performance of *Emotions* didn't even come close to that of *Mariah Carey,* ending up with a total of 3 million copies sold. While that might have seemed like a disappointment, it really wasn't. Out of the thousands of albums released each year—even those by established, name artists—very, very few sell enough to dent the charts, even its lower rungs. To go gold (that is, to sell half a million copies) is a great achievement; to go beyond that, to platinum (one million copies sold), is rare; past that point, an album is far more than successful—it's a skyrocket.

It should also be remembered that the sales of *Mariah Carey* were helped by a very skillful marketing campaign, which was absent for *Emotions*. This record sold on Mariah's popularity, the success of its singles, and most importantly, its own merit. Given those factors, it was an unqualified smash. The record led off with the title track, already familiar from its position as a number 1 single. Over a frothy groove that owed far more to seventies disco than nineties dance music, Mariah gave a joyful lyric. She used the high end of her range, but its presence, while more reserved, was also stronger and a fully integrated part of the song's arrangement, where it had seemed like an ornament before. This track was actually one of only two Carey-Cole-Clivilles compositions (the two other, faster tunes were credited to just Carey and Cole). As on all the other faster songs, David Cole played the keyboards, while Robert Clivilles contributed drums for a wonderfully bouncy feel (as on *Mariah Carey,* most of the instruments on this release were synthesized).

"And You Don't Remember" allowed Mariah's gospel side to show. Gliding silkily over organ chord changes, and rising to a heartbroken, much rawer chorus, the sad melody reflected the words—a story of being duped and then forgotten by a boyfriend, one of those men who obviously promises the world, then immediately goes on to the next girl. These two opening tracks showed that this album, for all its nineties instrumentation and technology, was going to achieve what Mariah had hoped. It would have a sixties and seventies feel—not only the songs themselves, but the way they were performed. Except for three cuts where Mariah had collaborated with others, she was entirely responsible for all the vocal arrangements (she'd worked with her coproducers on the instrumental arrangements). It was here, more than anywhere, that her influence showed—in the backgrounds, with their sweet, high harmonies that recalled black church choirs or the enthusiastic sounds of the young Motown ballads.

"Can't Let Go" was a pure, sad ballad, a pop song that could easily have been written in any decade from the fifties onward, but that also had a hymnlike quality in its minor-chord changes, particularly in the introduction. Not that that was a bad thing—with only twelve notes in the musical scale, by now almost every tune had been written. And for this, Mariah stayed with her huskier lower range, letting the emotion in her voice convey the pain above a simple instrumental backing.

For "Make It Happen," Mariah wrote a set of very autobiographical lyrics, dealing with the struggles she went through before being signed by Columbia (even down to the fact that she could only afford that single pair of holey sneakers!), and what kept her going through it all; her faith. That wasn't just a faith in herself and her talent, but also the ability to let herself go, to pray to God, and to trust in what would happen. These were, by far, her most inspiring words to date, letting others know that whatever they were doing, no matter how difficult things were, with help they could win through. Musically, the piece had a restrained dance beat, very Motownish, that owed more than a little to gospel, with a chorus—sung by Mariah, Trey, and Patrique—that rose gloriously from the verse to repeat and drive its very positive message home.

This was followed by what was probably the most anticipated song on the album, "If It's Over," the piece cowritten by Mariah and Carole King. It echoed the type of songs that had proved so powerful for Aretha Franklin in the late sixties—slow, but very soulful, and again, full of that gospel sound that Mariah loved. Such material allowed Mariah to really tear loose and show what she could do—which in reality was far more than the vocal gymnastics that seemed to comprise her reputation so far. From a deep rumble to a high wail, she covered five octaves wonderfully as the power of the tune built. The backing vocals—which once more had those churchy harmonies—filled out the spare melody, as did the stately horns, which entered toward the end. Indeed, the whole song was essentially a showcase for Mariah, and so beautifully out of time on a modern album that it came across as something quite new. It also showed that further collaborations between Mariah and Carole would be quite in order, and more than welcome. But no reprise would ever happen.

"You're So Cold" seemed to come across as four parts Emotions (the group) and one part Paula Abdul, the dancer-turned-singer who had some success before abruptly vanishing from the music scene. From a grandiose piano-and-vocal introduction, the song sailed into the chorus, driven throughout by David Cole's house-y piano work, the bubbly, snaking rhythm belying the angry lyrics, the upbeat tone of voice. Once more, this didn't quite seem like a nineties song, but rather like something that wouldn't have been out of place in the early disco era, and certainly a pleasant relief from the bass-heavy hip-hop that was filling the radio. The first song that Mariah and David penned together, "You're So Cold" had been considered as the album's lead single, but was eventually dropped in favor of "Emotions" and remained just an album track.

"So Blessed" was a sweet, touching song that displayed Mariah's softer side. Its tune recalled both fifties pop ballads and the soul changes of songs like "When a Man Loves a Woman," as it glided over layers of Hammond organ and synthesized strings. The joyful, glad words found their expression in Mariah's smooth, restrained singing, which sounded as if she were performing with a happy smile on her face.

"To Be Around You" was far more staccato. In his *Rolling Stone* review, Rob Tannenbaum accused David Cole of using "pumping house keyboards," but not too much of that had really been in evidence on *Emotions'* faster tracks, and certainly not here. He did, however, also remark that some material appeared to "recycle the chords of Cheryl Lynn's 'Got to Be Real.' " While this song paid tribute to Lynn's in its overall feel and arrangement, there were no real recycling and rewriting involved. With the spoken voices at the end, this track had an uplifting party sense, a sense of well-being that the words (about an attentive lover) conjured up.

The quiet changes of "Till the End of Time," with its gentle, almost lullaby melody, gave the impression that it was the final track, the winding-down of a night. It was a love song, directed at a boyfriend, but with the overall impression that Mariah was actually saying it to herself, rather than to him in the flesh. As it was, it worked perfectly as a segue between the rest of the album and its actual last cut, "The Wind."

"The Wind" was originally a jazz instrumental, written by Russell Freeman in the 1950s, which Walter Afanasieff had discovered on a record by the pianist Keith Jarrett. When Walter played it for Mariah, the melody touched her, inspiring a gorgeous set of lyrics about a friend who had died in a drunk-driving accident.

Musically, it was the greatest challenge she'd yet undertaken. She'd mastered gospel, but jazz, with its slippery chords and tumbling changes, was altogether a different matter. It required a subtle touch and, to put the emotions of this particular set of words across, a great deal of delicacy. Mariah handled it superbly, holding back, and moving to the swing of the beat, letting it direct her and not trying to push it. The piece also gave Walter a rare chance to shine, embellishing the vocal with runs on piano and synthesized vibes. The whispery vocal mingled with the instruments to create a melancholy mood that became the perfect closer, something to surprise listeners (as "Vanishing" had done on her debut) and to impress them, making it clear that, if she wanted, in time Mariah could have a strong future as a jazz singer.

More than anything, what *Emotions* showed was Mariah's remarkable consistency. *Mariah Carey* hadn't been a fluke; she was a reliable, professional performer, one who could deliver the goods in any style. It also demonstrated not just that she'd grown, but how much. Her progress was little short of remarkable. The material might have been of the same kind as the first album, but there was a great deal more finesse in everything—from the writing, through the arrangements, to the singing. She'd written exactly what she wanted, and her fans saw that. The fact that the album's highest chart position was number 4 was immaterial. As a portrait of Mariah as an artist coming into bloom, it was everything anyone could have hoped for.

Walter Afanasieff thought it truly captured Mariah at that time. "Her heart and soul [are] all over this record," he said, adding, "she developed a wisdom and professionalism that goes beyond her twenty-one years," a trait he attributed to her recent experiences, which he felt lent her the focus that was apparent on this record. He was of the belief that "new pop singers are going to want to emulate Mariah."

As with the first album, Mariah was loath to promote *Emotions* with public appearances. Except in one instance. She did perform on the 1991 MTV Video Music Awards. Onstage she came across relaxed and smiling, as if being there were second nature to her, quite a change from the year before when she'd complained of nervousness and shown no desire to play to live audiences. There was still no tour booked, but at least she'd made a small step in the right direction.

THE VIDEOS FOR the singles did eventually find commercial release, appended to the video of Mariah's "MTV Unplugged" appearance. The clips were preceded by an interview with Mariah (accompanied by her Doberman pinscher, Princess, and her cats Ninja and Thompkins), in which she talked about her experiences making the two albums back-to-back, which made them seem like one long album to her. She also discussed what she saw ahead for herself.

The "Make It Happen" video was directed by Marcus Nispel, who picked up on the gospel element of the song and used it as the focal point, having Mariah perform her song at a benefit to "Save Our Church." The audience, as they filed into a dusty, deserted building, was made up of the widest cross section possible: old and young (with a strong emphasis on children), abled and disabled, all races and colors. Although they were there for a good cause, everyone was out to have fun. From the first beat, dancers were moving. There was a deliberately amateurish, spontaneous quality about things, from the old-fashioned square microphone (Mariah's prop in the ads for her first album, as well as in the "Vision of Love" video), to the small drum kit and beat-up piano. Cuts to faces in the growing crowd showed people enjoying themselves, as well as a contented look on the face of the black minister, holding a little girl. The numbers onstage grew, too, as Mariah was joined by children playing cellos and a group of black women singing backup. At the end, when the song finished, there were real cheers—not on the record, but dubbed in to give more of a real, live experience to the video.

"Can't Let Go," Jim Sonzero's first work with Mariah, was a beautifully lush piece of work, full of surprising and imaginative camera angles. Filmed in black and white and in a muted focus, it was framed by its opening and closing shots, first of a pair of hands opening to reveal a white rose and, then, at the end, closing over it again. Mariah was in the courtyard of a house, strongly lit to create large variances of light and shadow. With her hair up and wearing a short black dress, she sang as the lens cut to images—flowers, a letter on a desk, the lines of a venetian blind—over her words. Quite often, the way the images were juxtaposed made it difficult for a second or two for the viewer to distinguish what was being filmed. And that was a good thing; it held the viewer's attention. For such a lonely song, it worked beautifully. This style had been attempted before, but rarely had it been done so well.

For "Emotions," director Jim Preiss honed in on the party element of the song and used that as his idea, reproduced here in the tune's "extended" version. The colors were toned down—blue for the interior scenes, brown (simulating firelight) for the evening fun outdoors—and even the daytime exteriors had a blurred, undefined edge to them.

The opening shots showed Mariah, wearing a wrap over a fifties-style bikini, in the backseat of a convertible, singing as the couple in the front seat conversed. From there, it cut to the party scenes, which took place in an old house. Inside, people were dancing, looking through records, and talking. A bush baby, someone's pet, wandered around lazily, big-eyed and curious. Outside, later, the party had heated up. Couples—black and white—were dancing and having fun. Notably, no one was shown drinking or using any kind of drugs, not even tobacco. Throughout, Mariah was singing, to no one in particular, which emphasized the overall sense of joy in the song. And even more than on the record (although it was exactly the same track), the high notes worked. They seemed to punctuate the fun perfectly.

Then, at the very end of the tape, just before the credits, there was some home-movie footage of Mariah: running on the beach with Princess, swimming, signing autographs in a record store. Her voice ran over the pictures, thanking the fans who'd helped her along the way with their support, their letters. It was a simple gesture, but one most artists wouldn't have thought to make, one that reinforced the idea that Mariah was truly a lady.

THE RELEASE OF the second album didn't foster any more malicious gossip about Mariah being a white girl trying to sound black. It appeared as if the greater gospel and soul influences in her sound had managed to erase all that.

Unfortunately, one piece of gossip that Mariah had been unable to dispel was that she was having a romance with Tommy Mottola. Although he'd long refuted it and she'd more or less done the same ("I read that stuff and I throw it away"), the rumors continued. Mariah refused to talk about it; she would neither confirm nor deny anything. The closest she came to any kind of statement was in an interview with *USA Today,* when, asked if she had a boyfriend, she answered, "Sort of, but I'd rather not get into it."

Emotions ended a long, intense period of work for Mariah. Two years with virtually no break and the cycle of writing, recording, promoting, writing, recording, and promoting yet again can leave a person exhausted. With her first album, Mariah had had to establish herself, make her name. That done—and done very, very successfully—on the second, she had to show that *she* was at the heart of everything, that she wasn't just another good singer who allowed herself to be shaped by the producers and her material. And *Emotions* had certainly proved that. In taking greater responsibility for the album, Mariah took on a challenge which she more than met head-on. She could write and sing in a variety of styles, she'd fully absorbed her influences, and she wasn't afraid to try to expand her musical range (as on "The Wind"). *Mariah Carey* was the record of a young woman quickly beginning to maturate as an artist. (*Emotions* did garner one Grammy nomination, a joint one for Mariah and Walter Afanasieff as producers. But at the 1992 ceremony, it failed to win.)

More than that, Mariah had managed her career with both style and dignity—and without hogging the spotlight. Other artists courted the crowds and treated controversy like a close friend. Mariah wasn't one of them. Yes, she made videos and was featured in them, but that was virtually an extension of making records. In reality, she was more than happy to let the music speak for itself, and she would very likely have been content to leave it at that and never make another public singing appearance.

And so Mariah reached the end of one era. She'd grown tremendously, both artistically and personally, and had gone almost before our eyes from a girl to a woman, one who was both lovely and talented. Even if she never released another album, she'd made her mark, and she would have a lasting place in the record books for her string of number 1 hits. But Mariah liked to stare challenges in the face, and the next one was just around the corner.

5

The next problem in Mariah's life came from an unexpected source: her stepfather, Joseph Vian, who'd married Patricia Carey in 1987, just before Mariah left home to seek her fame and fortune in Manhattan.

By early 1992, Vian and Patricia had split up; their divorce would become final later that year. Meanwhile, however, Vian had begun proceedings against Mariah in Federal District Court in New York. He charged that Mariah "agreed orally that he would have a license to market singing dolls in her likeness." He made other claims as well, including one that Mariah "was unjustly enriched at his expense in that he contributed to her support and to the development of her professional career, with the expectation of reward." This ran entirely counter to Mariah's story that her mother would have bought her another pair of shoes to replace the holey sneakers she lived in for a year, but she preferred to be self-supporting. But perhaps the harshest blow was Vian's allegation that Mariah "intentionally and/or negligently . . . interfered in his relationship with his wife, defendant's mother, destroying that relationship and causing him to fall into a deep depression from which he has not recovered."

Whether Mariah liked Vian or not, the closeness of her relationship with her mother had been well established and was never in doubt. It seemed very unlikely that Mariah would do anything to bring unhappiness to Patricia; on the contrary, she'd have been far more likely to have done what she could to make her mother happier. The Federal District Court judge obviously agreed, because later in the year he dismissed both that claim and others, including the allegation that Mariah unjustly enriched herself at Vian's expense.

As for the "Mariah dolls," it would be nearly a year before that case was settled. Mariah, testifying by deposition, explained that she thought Vian's comments about the dolls were a joke. In April 1993, Judge Michael B. Mukasey dismissed the charge, stating, "In sum, [Vian] has not raised a triable issue of fact as to the existence of a contract." The judge continued, "Viewing the facts in the light most favorable to [Vian], as I have done in deciding this motion, there is no evidence that [Carey] thought, or should have thought, that [he] was serious about entering into a contract, nor that she believed she had bound herself to a licensing agreement for 'Mariah dolls' by saying 'Okay' and nodding her head when her stepfather made passing references to the idea. . . ." Mukasey eventually concluded, "Even if the plaintiff had a valid contract, which I stress again he did not, he has not alleged recoverable damages." In essence, this was a reprimand for Vian, who was going away with nothing—except bad feelings and, of course, none of the money that Mariah had made by her own talent.

THE BREAK THAT Mariah took from music proved to be very short, as might be expected from such a workaholic personality. She knew she needed to take her songs to the fans. After all, they'd bought millions of her albums and singles. But, as she'd said, she didn't want to undertake a concert tour. The solution came in the form of a television program.

MTV's "Unplugged" had been on the air for quite a few years before it became popular. Originally hosted by singer/songwriter Jules Shear ("If She Knew What She Wants"), it had been intended to provide an informal, live setting for musicians to offer very basic versions of their songs and to sit in with other artists. That particular idea didn't seem to draw an audience, so the concept was revamped. Shear was dropped, and a greater concentration was placed on bringing in "name" artists, who would in turn attract more viewers. The idea proved phenomenally successful. Suddenly, the concept of playing "unplugged" was everywhere— not only on television, but also in clubs. However, "Unplugged" wasn't quite as stripped down as its name implied. Whole bands appeared on the show, and it was common to see drum kits and keyboards on the stage, with the groups performing just straight "acoustic" versions of their hits. Some, like LL Cool J, were more adventurous, offering rap freed from its samples and electric back- drop. But most, like Eric Clapton, were content to take the easy route, which ended up more bland than basic.

For Mariah, "Unplugged" was ideal. She would be seen by large numbers of people with cable TV—not only fans, but also the curious. By performing live, she would be able to dispel any thoughts that she was a "manufactured" artist. And, most impor- tant, working in this form would offer her a challenge, something she could never resist. On Mariah's recordings, most of the instru- mental backing for her voice had been provided by synthesizers and drum machines. An acoustic setting, however, would require working with real musicians and singers; how could she turn it down?

The answer, obviously, was that she couldn't. And she didn't.

THE PROBLEMS MARIAH and Walter Afanasieff (by now her co- arranger of choice) faced were twofold. First, what material should they pick? And then, how should they present it?

Mariah's big hits were what most people were familiar with— the songs they'd heard on the radio, with infectious choruses they could sing in their sleep. On the other hand, less familiar material, like "Vanishing" and "The Wind," had great possibilities for a show like "Unplugged." In the end, Mariah and Walter decided to go with the popular tunes. It was a decision that made perfect sense for Mariah's big television debut (yes, she'd been on "Saturday Night Live" and "Arsenio Hall," but this would be *her* show); she would be giving people what they really wanted to hear.

As for the presentation, that raised a number of possibilities. Straight renditions of the songs with acoustic instruments would probably be fine, and would satisfy the public. But there was no real challenge in that. It didn't do anything new. Instead, Mariah fell back on her old loves, gospel and soul music. While the rumors of "another white girl singing black" seemed to have died down with the release of *Emotions,* this would banish them completely.

Making preparations for the taping was a time-consuming venture. There was a great deal to be done before any rehearsals could be undertaken. Using real musicians as opposed to electronics necessitated bringing in both a string and a brass section, as well as piano, guitars, drums, and backing singers. Parts had to be written for all these people, and with the emphasis on Mariah's gospel and soul sides, these parts couldn't just duplicate the arrangements on the albums.

After this came the rehearsals, a difficult proposition with so many people, even if they were all top-notch musicians.

And finally, everything had to be sorted out in the studio. The idea of the program might be to be unplugged, but the reality involved a large number of microphones, a very carefully mixed sound, camera angles to be worked out, stage positions for all the performers. Plus there was Mariah's often-stated goal of perfection in everything. Which meant that the show's production crew faced a nightmare. Luckily, some of the technical staff were people who'd worked with Mariah before. The mixing was handled by Dana Jon Chappelle, who'd handled exactly that job on both her albums, and the show's director was Larry Jordan, who had performed the same job on the "Someday" video. All in all, a crew of ten was needed to record the show.

But that wasn't all. "[P]eople kept saying to do an oldie," Mariah said. "Two nights before the actual show I decided on 'I'll Be There' " (a number 1 hit for the Jackson Five which stayed at the top of the charts for five weeks). This, of course, only added to the problems. It meant another song to hurriedly arrange and learn—and to cause the crew headaches.

The taping took place before an invited audience at the Kaufman Astoria Studios in New York on March 16, 1992, eleven days before Mariah's twenty-second birthday. The audience was ready for her, and cheers greeted Mariah as she opened her mouth to sing the first notes of "Emotions." Dressed all in black—as was almost everyone else crowded onto the stage—in a short jacket, leotard, tight jeans, and boots—she was also ready for them.

As any fan might have predicted, it was a gospelish introduction. Sitting in on piano, guest David Cole (the only one not completely in black; he wore a sparkling silver jacket) held the chords behind the voices, letting it all build before the beat kicked in and everyone got to work.

Mariah had a small triangle of stage to herself, nearest the crowd. Everyone else was cramped. A four-piece string section (Belinda Whitney Barnett, Cecilia Hobbs-Gardner, Wince Garvey, and Laura Corcos) sat off to the side in front of San Shea, who'd worked out the string arrangements and was playing the harpsichord and harmonium. The rhythm section held the back of the stage—Gigi Conway on drums, Randy Jackson on bass, Vernon Black on guitar, and two percussionists, Sammy Figueroa and Ren Klyce, who contributed timpanis, celeste, and tubular and orchestral bells. The other side of the stage was reserved for the "Saturday Night Live" horns (Lew Delgatto, baritone saxophone; Lenny Pickett, tenor saxophone; George Young, alto saxophone; Earl Gardner, trumpet; and Steve Turre, trombone), who would appear on one song.

In the past, Mariah had referred to her music as "vocally driven," and the number of backup singers she surrounded herself with here really proved she meant it. There were ten of them clustered around the piano. Quite naturally, they were led by her longtime associates Trey Lorenz and Patrique McMillan, with the addition of Geno Morris and the Darryl Douglass Workshop Company (Kelly Price, Cheree Price, Melanie Daniels, Peggy Harley, Liz Stewart, Spencer Washington, and Henry Casper). By the first chorus of the opening song, they'd proved their worth. They added the warmth of a Baptist choir, weaving in and out behind Mariah's voice and working with it to create the melody over the rhythm. In this context, "Emotions," though the same tune and the same words, sounded quite different—it was much rawer and earthier, two qualities Mariah had wanted in her music from the time of her debut record. David Cole had the right touch, adding notes and fills that accentuated the feel. Mariah touched her high notes perfectly, and when the instruments cut out before the song's end, leaving just the voices, it seemed as it should be. Many in the studio would probably have been quite content to have had a whole show of just voices!

The audience had been clapping along with the beat from the start, and would do so for all the up-tempo material. One small, particularly active group was dancing and waving behind the stage.

It all felt right, as if this was the perfect way to see Mariah Carey. If she appeared nervous at first, standing by the microphone, she overcame it very quickly, walking around, singing to the crowd and the camera. As the song ended and the applause began, she giggled. Only she knew what reaction she'd been expecting, but this outpouring seemed to surprise and gratify her. There were still some jitters in her, of course—that was only to be expected, and she expressed them as giggles—but she truly appreciated these fans, thanking them after every piece, and their reception helped her slowly relax over the course of the taping.

After the first song, "the incredible" Walter Afanasieff replaced David Cole at the piano, and the "Saturday Night Live" horns took the stage to perform the tune Mariah had written with "one of my idols"—Carole King. The recorded version of "If It's Over" had a Southern soul feel—the kind that filled material which came out on the Stax label in the late sixties—which really mixed soul and gospel. But this version truly captured that idea. And with the additional voices, it could almost have been recorded in church.

This made it quite clear that not only had Mariah and Walter (who co-arranged the material for this show) broken "the arrangements down to their simplest forms by using only acoustic instruments," they'd in fact done much more. This style perfectly suited both Mariah's voice and her songs, and the interaction with other musicians, as opposed to synthesizers, added a warmth to the music that made it more immediate and alive.

"If It's Over," with its lazy rhythm and stop-time pause beats, served Mariah's lower register well, although on the vocal "breakdown" at the crescendo, she couldn't resist letting the octaves soar briefly skyward.

However, it was impossible not to note the stylistic differences at the keyboard between Walter Afanasieff and David Cole. Cole was much freer in his playing, and he was able to concentrate on his playing alone. Walter's style was more formal, and he also had to lead an entire band of twenty-six, who looked to him for their musical cues. For the specifically gospel-style performance Mariah was giving, Cole (or someone like him) was a much more suitable performer. That wasn't to take away from Afanasieff's talent by any means; his gift was obvious, and his empathy with Mariah had worked very well for both of them. And, for ballads, he had an ideal style: subdued, playing to the voice rather than around it. But this particular type of live performance needed a more outgoing style, one which led rather than followed.

This really showed on the next song, "Someday." Cole's churchy stylings could have added a great deal to it. Not that Afanasieff's was a bad version; not by any means. It percolated well, with the voices bouncing over the rhythm section. And it gave Mariah a real chance to show off her vocal gymnastics. But the spark that could have turned something good into something really special never quite caught. However, for the audience it was just fine, as they were very happily caught up in the moment, clapping to the beat. And even Mariah herself seemed happy with it, turning to exchange smiles with the others.

When it was over, Mariah said it was the last time she would be needing to use the top end of her range for the evening, for which she seemed quite glad, even though she'd been quite sparing with it so far, making it a necessary part of the songs, rather than a twist or a gimmick. Live, to be able to hear herself, she needed to block one ear with a hand or finger. This technique, common among folksingers, enables the singer to get an accurate gauge of pitch. One can only assume that all the sophisticated electronics used on the show, including the monitors (small speakers facing the performers that allowed them to hear everybody else onstage), didn't do a very good job of broadcasting high frequencies.

When things slowed down a little for what to many was still Mariah's "big hit," "Vision of Love," she had a chance to perch on a stool. For such an inexperienced live performer, she'd held control of the audience remarkably well, and this immediately recognizable piece was the last step needed to cement the bond.

Again, with Mariah being able to play off all the other voices, and with its swaying, lulling rhythm, the song came across as quite fresh, without the Top Forty gloss that had characterized the single. As with all Mariah's material, such rawness suited it, giving it a kick of emotion and, once more, a gospelish edge that pointed out the hopefulness of the lyrics. And, by sticking with her lower registers, Mariah was able to offer a throatier performance. (Interestingly, as she's moved further from her debut, with its high notes that helped to make her name known, Mariah has kept more and more to her lower register, allowing her singing technique, rather than any ornament, to shine.)

For "Make It Happen," David Cole returned to the stage to duet with Walter Afanasieff on the piano. He took the right-hand, or treble parts, while Walter supplied the underpinning, or bass parts. Cole's energy was quite infectious, his big smile shining as much as any of the stage lights as he bounced to the beat on the piano stool. This pairing illustrated perfectly the difference in the two men's styles. Cole brought the song alive, filling in with little runs, working against the beat on the chorus, giving it the fire that "Someday" never quite managed, even animating Walter to move with him. His innate feel for this kind of music shone through in his playing. It might have been simple, but every note was effective.

All the vocalists obviously caught this, too, for they sang just like a church choir ("Make It Happen" was, in its own way, a song of praise), letting the repeated choruses build behind Mariah, giving her a chance to wail and solo, not like any pop diva performing for a crowd, but like someone filled with the spirit. The roughness of this version succeeded in a way the recorded version on *Emotions* could never manage. In the sterile atmosphere of a studio, where perfection, technology, and overdubbing were the rules, spontaneity had no place. On the stage, it was valued, and this performance had it. Everyone pushed everyone else just a little further, to create something wonderful, and judging by the response, the audience realized it, as did Mariah when the song was finished. It was a rare moment, one that true performers strive for and don't find often enough to satisfy themselves.

It was followed by another rare moment, the hastily assembled adaptation of the Jackson Five's "I'll Be There." The way Walter and Mariah had arranged the song, she took the Michael Jackson lead, and Trey Lorenz, with his high, sweet voice, took what had originally been Jermaine Jackson's part, the second lead. After two years of working with Mariah, Trey was getting his chance to shine, and outfitted in a worn black leather motorcycle jacket and a baseball cap, he looked ready for it.

It was interesting that with so many songs of her own, Mariah chose to cover a tune that was more than twenty years old. As a bit of fun, or as a tribute to the Jacksons, it was a good idea. But almost certainly no one could have predicted the impact this particular performance would have. As good as everything so far had been—and it had been exceptional—suddenly giving Mariah a reputation as a live performer that would have been difficult for anyone, let alone a rookie, to live up to, this song now propelled it into the stratosphere.

On the surface, there was nothing remarkable about it. The song had been covered many times over the years, by any number of people. Maybe it was the friendship between Mariah and Trey, or maybe it was the atmosphere that was in the studio that night. Whatever the cause, it brought out something amazing in both singers and started Trey Lorenz on a well-earned solo career.

With such a short preparation time, the instrumental arrangement was very basic, just a simple backing for the voices, all of which backed Mariah on the verses. When she introduced Trey for his part, he seemed bashful at first, but then he dove into the role and sang his heart out. The first time around, he stuck to the melody, giving a lovely counterpoint to Mariah's alto. But, on his second chance, he climaxed by soaring into the high, unbelievable falsetto that had first made Mariah take notice of him in the recording studio. It was another of those perfect moments, and everyone knew it, performers and audience alike. Although her performance was equally tender, Mariah seemed quite content to hold back and let Trey bask in the spotlight.

Later, he would be unable to recall his performance, which he didn't hear for a few months after the taping. "[G]reat goodness, I *think* we were singing really good that day, but I wasn't so sure about me. I was really relieved when I listened."

All too often today, concerts bring standing ovations followed by planned encores. Mariah and Trey's rendition of "I'll Be There" literally brought the crowd out of their seats, clapping and cheering, an accolade that was honestly earned.

After that, almost anything would have come as an anticlimax. So the show ended on a low-key note, with "Can't Let Go," which saw Mariah backed only by piano, percussion, bass, and voices. It was, she insisted, an off-the-cuff performance of the song, the arrangement made up as they went along, but it seems likely that there was at least *some* rehearsal, however perfunctory, for it to work that well. This really was a song stripped to its basics, quite raw, which only served to increase its appeal. The lyrics, which were full of heartbreak and confusion, truly came across with complete vulnerability (a tribute to Mariah's vocal ability), and her brief swoop through the upper register just before the song's close gave it a wonderful, if unexpected, conclusion.

Needless to say, the crowd, which had been utterly won over from the beginning, was ecstatic. Mariah herself, to judge from her grin, was pleased with the way things had gone. A show, particularly one with so many musicians, involved a great deal of rehearsal, and the sessions for this had gone quickly and had been intense. She was lucky in that a number of the participants had worked with her on her albums and were therefore familiar with much of the material. And the rest were experienced session musicians. But even then, mistakes could happen. For this, though, none did; in fact, things couldn't have gone any better.

It was also a learning experience for Mariah: " 'Unplugged' taught me a lot about myself because I tend to nitpick everything I do and make it a little too perfect because I'm a perfectionist," she told *Billboard*'s Melinda Newman. "I'll always go over the raw stuff, and now I've gotten to the point where I understand that the raw stuff is usually better."

Originally, Mariah's "Unplugged" show was meant to simply be a telecast, to stand or fall on its own. It would air on MTV and that would be the end of things. No video, and most certainly no album, would follow; after all, *Emotions* was still doing well, having gone multi-platinum, and since the show was short and contained no real new material, there seemed to be no point in releasing it. Besides, Mariah and Walter were already hard at work, beginning to write songs for her third album, scheduled to appear sometime during 1993.

But public reaction has a power all its own, as had been shown by the way *Mariah Carey* and its singles sold, far beyond the possibilities or dreams of any record-company hype.

MTV usually aired each new "Unplugged" show a few times over the course of a month, then retired it to the vaults, to be dragged out and dusted off every once in a while. From the first time it was shown, though, Mariah's show proved almost unbelievably popular. Calls came in from all over the country, causing far more reruns of the performance than had been anticipated. Nor was it popular only with fans; critics, too, found much to praise in it. *Time*'s Christopher John Farley called it "deservedly acclaimed," and his words only echoed sentiment around the country. Upon the release of the show as an EP (an abbreviation for "extended play," a format which was very popular in the sixties, consisting of four tracks on a seven-inch vinyl disc, but which had since fallen out of favor), *Rolling Stone* reviewed it with Eric Clapton's MTV set, saying that Mariah's version of "I'll Be There" could easily be mistaken for the Jackson Five's, "and that's a mighty compliment." The reviewer was also enthusiastic about "Someday," "transformed into a bubbly gush of pure pop," and ended, "Carey bests Clapton in a battle of the bands? Only on MTV."

The groundswell was such that Columbia was more or less forced to issue the show. People wanted to play it at home, in their cars, wherever. And, more than anything, they wanted to listen to that version of "I'll Be There." So that was what the company gave them. *MTV Unplugged* came out as a reduced-price EP, because of its shorter length, and "I'll Be There" was released as a single.

Both were unsurprisingly successful. "I'll Be There" debuted on the Hot 100 at number 13, the highest entry yet for one of Mariah's songs. Probably not even Mariah could have dreamed that it would do so well, nor could she have imagined that such a hastily chosen and rehearsed cover song would give her a sixth number 1 hit. But it did, barely pausing on its way to the top of the charts. After four weeks, it was in the number 1 spot, after brief pauses at number 4 and number 2, and it stayed there for two weeks beginning June 20, 1992.

The EP debuted on the album charts the week the single reached number 1, coming in at number 8. The next week it rose to number 5, and then it peaked at number 3. Not as good a performance as "I'll Be There," but it was still far more than credible for a piece of work which wasn't even originally going to be released. It would go on to sell more than 2 million copies.

Mariah and Columbia Records decided to donate part of the proceeds from the *MTV Unplugged* EP to a number of charities: AmFAR (the American Foundation for AIDS Research), the United Negro College Fund, Hale House Center, Inc., and the T. J. Martell Foundation, another AIDS-related organization. It seemed only right; after all, they'd had a hit record given to them from something they'd never intended to release. But, still, it was a magnanimous gesture, and one that was rightly done with a minimum of publicity.

THE SUCCESS OF "I'll Be There" had a gratifying side effect. It gave Trey Lorenz a solo career. Epic (part of the Columbia family of labels and one-time home of Brenda K. Starr) signed him, not just on the strength of that one song, but also because of his own ability, as well as the other work he'd done with Mariah. Suddenly, the important thing was for Trey to get a good record out as soon as possible, before his name was forgotten.

It turned out that he had the best possible help. Mariah and Walter had been looking ahead to her new album but Mariah said, "I really didn't want all the fun and interest behind [Trey] with the 'I'll Be There' record to go to waste, so we just went at it for about three months." So, what had been a writing session for Mariah "became a Trey writing session instead. . . . I was really into the project."

In fact, she was so into it that she chose to produce or coproduce six tracks on Trey's album. On five of those, she worked with Walter Afanasieff. And they were not the only star talents employed in the production booth. There was Keith Thomas, who had worked with both Amy Grant and Vanessa Williams; Mark C. Rooney; Mark Morales; Glen Ballard (who'd go on to real fame and fortune with Alanis Morrissette); and BeBe Winans, part of the soul/gospel group the Winans.

Mariah cowrote two of the songs, which proved to be the most difficult for her to produce. "I'm sort of writing them as we go along," she said. "When you don't have a demo to refer to and you're doing the track, it's like, 'What am I going to sing on this line and how should the background go on this one?' as opposed to when someone has already written it and you just do it."

Quite naturally, the arrangements centered around Trey's vocals, with many of the vocal arrangements and backgrounds handled by Mariah, as well as by Will Downing, Audrey Wheeler, and Cindy Mizelle (who had appeared with Mariah on *Emotions*). The production experience triggered in Mariah the idea of perhaps producing other songs ("possibly a contemporary gospel" artist), although no names were mentioned, nor any time, and to date it hasn't happened.

However, this was *Trey's* big break. Mariah's involvement was important, both to the album having happened in the first place and to its future success, but in the end it all came down to Trey and the work he'd put in over the years. His musical career hadn't begun with Mariah—very far from it. In fact, he'd been involved with music for most of his life, singing in church in Florence, South Carolina, with his parents, and then taking piano lessons before joining the Players, a Top 40 band, on vocals and keyboards, and having a brief fling with a group called Squeak and the Deep while majoring in advertising at Fairleigh Dickinson University.

Trey Lorenz was preceded by a single, "Someone to Hold." If it didn't have quite the impact on the charts that Mariah's first single had, it still sold more than respectably, climbing through chart positions in the thirties all the way to the teens before falling again. Not at all bad for a former backup singer! Its success certainly helped pull the album along on its release, giving it a chance to crack the Top Fifty.

Mariah took a great deal of pride in her protégé's acceptance by the record-buying public. "I'm trying not to talk too much and let the music speak for itself, but I think people are ready to hear him." And obviously they were, from the way his solo career was launched. Having pushed Trey out of the nest and seen him fly, though, Mariah didn't end her involvement with him. Trey didn't sing on the *Music Box* album, but he did sing on Mariah's television special. He also opened the concert she performed as part of her tour on December 2, 1993, at the Spectrum in Philadelphia, giving him the chance to perform live before a large group of people. And he'd return to help out in a small way on *Butterfly.*

OF COURSE, SIMPLY releasing the EP couldn't be the sum total of Columbia's effort with Mariah's "Unplugged" show. With large numbers of people—and Mariah Carey fans—throughout the country having no access to cable television, there was a very definite market for a video of the show. To forestall any possible bootlegging, Sony Music Video released it under the title *MTV Unplugged + 3.* Given that the performance itself only ran for half an hour, Columbia added the three videos from *Emotions,* which hadn't seen any previous commercial release; some backstage footage of Mariah rehearsing and performing on "Soul Train"; a short interview; and some black-and-white "home movie" footage. Put together this way, it made a very nice package, a present for old fans and new converts alike. Those who'd discovered Mariah's music through the "Unplugged" show heard a sampling of album material, which contrasted the rawness of the live experience with studio polish.

The most important aspect of the "Unplugged" show wasn't the record and video sales it ended up generating, but rather that it proved Mariah to be an extremely valid live performer, one who had a very sure sense of the direction she wanted her live show to take. Whenever she finally did decide to tour—which at this point was still not even being considered—she would be able to undertake the venture with a great deal more confidence. And while Mariah might not be able to recreate the close feeling of her "Unplugged" show—when she toured, she would be playing stadiums and large theaters—she had quite firmly shown what she was capable of doing.

But, far more than that, it put her in control of her own music. Not that she hadn't had any control before. After all, it would be difficult not to have some control when you're the singer, cocomposer, co-arranger, and coproducer. By this time, though, Mariah had found her audience and established herself with a very strong fan base, and she could afford to indulge her tastes a little. That was the feeling that came across in the "Unplugged" show—that its direction originated very much with Mariah. On her first album, she'd taken suggestions from Columbia (albeit grudgingly on occasion, having firm ideas of her own), admitting that it was their money. *Emotions* had more of her in every part of it, but it was only a stop on the road to "Unplugged," her proving ground.

How much influence this performance would carry on Mariah's next record would still have to be seen. The fact that public demand caused the release of *Unplugged* as an EP, coupled with the commercial success of such a project, suggested that her ideas would now carry a great deal of weight. Much would depend on the type of songs she and Walter had been writing. Another factor to be considered was Mariah's production work for Trey Lorenz, which opened her eyes to a large number of studio possibilities.

But all of that lay in the future. Mariah was certainly due a good rest by now, away from the grind of recording and promotion. For three and a half years, that had been her life, day in and day out, and while it had documented her remarkable growth as an artist, even an artist can burn out. Besides, it had given Mariah very little time to enjoy any kind of life of her own. While she might have dreamed about music when other girls dreamed of marriage, those dreams had been more than adequately filled by now, not only as a performer and songwriter, but finally as a producer of someone else.

The writing for the next album would continue, of course. Mariah, after all, was a woman who would call her answering service to hum a line for a new song or note a fragment of a lyric.

But at least the whole—the writing, recording, mixing of the record—could now be taken at a more relaxed, more sensible pace.

After having given her fans a great deal of music over the last three years, Mariah could afford to take a year or more between albums without it seeming as if she'd ever been away. She was still one of the (if not *the*) leading pop divas, and there were no new-comers on the horizon, no pretenders to the throne waiting around the corner. It remained, as it had been in 1990 when *Mariah Carey* was released, Mariah and Whitney.

SUCH WAS THE nature of mainstream pop in the early nineties; it was more or less static. The same few names tended to crop up again and again: Mariah, Whitney, Phil Collins, Billy Joel, and a few others. These were the artists who would be perennially pop-ular, not only with the young, but with all age groups. What had changed was the huge public acceptance of both rap and alterna-tive music. The impact they'd made was felt not only in the album charts, an area one might expect, but also in the Hot 100. Rap acts were making the Top Twenty with astonishing regularity. Rap fashions became the norm for a whole set of teenagers, while an-other set, inspired by the whole "Seattle sound" (the catalyst for the popularity of "alternative music"), settled into the plaid flannel and torn jeans of grunge chic.

Alternative music would not affect Mariah's record sales. A Mariah Carey fan would be unlikely to be interested in the latest Nirvana record, and vice versa. And, unlike Whitney Houston—whose records, interestingly, suddenly seemed to be more heavily weighted toward ballads—Mariah's dance material at this stage owed far more to soul and disco than to any current hip-hop trend. Not that she didn't like hip-hop, but at the moment, it didn't fit with either her music or the image Columbia wanted for her. Be-sides, went the thinking, paying less attention to fads would yield another long-term dividend; timelessness never went out of style.

It would place her in a continuum that encompassed the best of singers—the Streisands, Sinatras, and Holidays—no bad thing in itself, and a big asset to a young singer with many productive years ahead of her. And it was definitely appreciated by the public who, in February 1993, added to Mariah's awards shelf two American Music Awards. This gave a boost to her sales: the *Unplugged* EP rose back to number 44 from number 71 a week later.

IN HER HIGH-SCHOOL yearbook, Mariah had listed her interests as sleeping late, Corvettes, and "guiedos" [sic]. Well, these days she could afford a new (or vintage, for that matter) Corvette for every day of the month, if not the year, and she could sleep until whatever time she chose, with no one to tell her she was being lazy.

Which left one thing.

From the beginning of her climb to superstardom, Mariah had been very reluctant to talk about any romance in her life, to the point of secrecy. It wasn't part of the business, and that made it hers and hers alone. All the rumors that circulated about Mariah and Tommy Mottola (of Italian descent), she dismissed out of hand.

But it wouldn't be long before the whole world had a chance to learn what was really going on in Mariah's private life, and to share her joy in it.

6

A lot of young women get disillusioned looking for Mr. right. He never shows up in most cases. But in my case, yes!"

That was the way Mariah talked about her romance and upcoming marriage, when she finally was willing to open up about it. Actually, it wasn't really a case of being willing to open up. It was rather that she couldn't keep it a secret any longer, not after a wedding date had been set and all the arrangements had been set in motion.

So who was the lucky man?

Tommy Mottola.

Despite all their denials, the rumors had continued, even if they'd died down somewhat after the *Emotions* album. In all fairness, the couple had been incredibly discreet. No pictures of the two of them together had been published in any of the tabloids, nothing that would even have begun to tarnish the reputation of either one. Tommy was divorced, his settlement final after a fairly bitter court fight in 1991. And Mariah had no previous ties. There were a few reports of boyfriends in the past, but nothing more serious than a high-school romance. This, on the other hand, was the real thing.

Not too surprisingly, this love match had begun after Tommy signed Mariah to Columbia. At first, everything was completely businesslike, but that changed while she was making *Mariah Carey* (during which time Tommy separated from his wife). "It just sort of happened," Mariah said. "We had a lot in common, and we just gradually came together."

The need for secrecy was obvious. At the time, Tommy was the head of her record company, quite possibly the single most influential record executive in the United States. He had discovered Mariah, brought her to Columbia, and for all intents and purposes, he had been her mentor, guiding her career—at least in the beginning. On *Mariah Carey* and *Emotions,* he had received executive-producer credit. If their burgeoning romance had truly become public, things would have been a little difficult for Tommy Mottola; the way he had been pushing her could easily have been viewed as a case of conflict of interest. And, with his separation and divorce so recent, Mariah might well have ended up being tagged the "other woman," which might have seemed outdated these days, but which still carried a large stigma with a lot of people.

At first, although there was a definite attraction between them, Mariah said, "I was so shell-shocked . . . I couldn't see anyone in a romantic light. But over the next few months as we began to work more closely our relationship changed and developed. It was a gradual, beautiful thing. I've now got the man of my dreams."

One other reason not to talk about it at all, Mariah said, was that it was better not to say anything "until we decided what we were going to do. He was pretty much my first serious boyfriend—I mean, anyone else was in my high school days."

There was one factor that made the pairing seem strange: Tommy was almost twenty years older than Mariah. While there have been many successful, happy unions with such an age gap, it remained unusual. However, Mariah insisted, "I don't focus on it. We don't look at each other with a big age difference. We are just right for each other, and that is all that matters. If you are really right for each other, that will shine through all the differences, everything—race and age." And, she added, "I don't think of Tommy as an older person. I think of him as a very special person. Everybody who knows us realizes we're right for each other."

Still, there would be a few small things that would highlight how many years stood between them.

Mariah admitted, "occasionally he'll know a song that I've never heard of, or I'll know songs that I'm like, 'Oh, this reminds me of seventh grade,' and it was, like, not that long ago."

But it still seemed odd. Mariah, so young and bouncy, with so much living to do, was a vegetarian with very strong views about her independence. And Mottola, whose daily life was consumed by business matters, was a collector of guns and a hunter. There were so many opposites. Still, as the old saying went, love conquers all, and it apparently had done so in this case.

"Tommy is just the greatest person," Mariah gushed to Steve Dougherty in *People* magazine. "He knows so much; he's funny. I can't imagine anybody else who would be so supportive and so understanding and helpful. He lifts me up." They were indisputably the words of a woman in love.

Even so, the fact that she was actually going to get married, to make such a huge commitment, seemed to surprise Mariah. "I never thought I would [get married] because my parents got divorced, and it gives you a different attitude about that sort of thing. It kind of hardens you; you know what I mean?" It was quite understandable. She'd seen the bad side. She had the deep memories of the fights, the tears, the pain, and she knew what it was like to grow up in what used to be called "a broken home." It would be enough to make anyone think twice about taking such a big step. Later, Mariah would admit that her friends were equally surprised by her move, half-expecting her to have an attack of cold feet before the wedding happened. "[E]verybody that knows me was freaked out that I actually did it. I think they thought I was going to run at the last minute."

But while preparations for her big day took up more and more of Mariah's time, they didn't fill it completely. There was still the small matter of her career. During 1992 and the early part of 1993, crammed in among her other obligations, Mariah and Walter Afanasieff (and others) had written the material for her next album, and she'd recorded it, using what had become her favorite studio for vocals, Right Track in New York, a place where she

Smile for the camera. That's great!

Reflecting on the new life

The joy of success

*On tour—Mariah at
Madison Square
Garden*

Giving it all to the music

Always a commanding presence on stage

Acknowledging the applause

"One Sweet Night" on stage

A new life, a new 'do

An open outlook on life

could just lose herself singing. "I love to go in and sing all the background parts and then hear like twenty tracks of my own voice coming back through the speaker," she said, describing the place where she felt happiest. By spring, the project had been completed, ready for release in the late summer or early fall, one of Columbia's big albums of the season, which would lead into Christmas and generate plenty of extra sales. After the fairly relaxed time of this record, things began getting hectic again as the wedding date loomed closer. As with almost all weddings in history, it was a case of "so much to do, so little time."

TRADITIONALLY, JUNE IS the month when brides walk down the aisle, and since Mariah had a wide streak of romanticism in her heart, she would be no exception. The couple named the day to the press and Mariah's fans: it would be June 5, 1993, a Saturday. But that would be the climax of all the work. Before the ceremony and reception, there was the service to plan (it would be a church wedding, in line with Mariah's traditional approach to things), the invitations to be sent, the gown and shoes to be designed, a never-ending list.

At least, in this modern age, Mariah was able to employ wedding consultants to take care of most of the work. Like every bride, she wanted her wedding day to be special. Unlike most of them, though, she had the money (not to mention the name) to make sure it would be. To be certain the press wouldn't spread all the details beforehand, some of the consultants, at least the ones dealing with what she would wear, had to sign four-page affidavits binding them to secrecy before they were employed.

Able to take her pick of designers, Mariah finally settled on Vera Wang, a well-known name in the fashion world who specialized in wedding dresses. The gown, it was decided, would be quite spectacular, befitting a young woman of Mariah's status.

What Mariah really wanted was a very traditional ceremony, like that enjoyed by Prince Charles and Lady Diana Spencer in

1981. That day, with its triumph of pomp and circumstance, was an inspiration to her. It was, of course, romantic.

Reports had her watching a tape of the royal wedding "over and over," getting the flavor of it and absorbing ideas. But that wasn't exactly the case, she'd insist later. "The ceremony was really traditional, so I wanted to look at examples of a traditional wedding to get some ideas. So I watched it, like, twice. I didn't sit at home with the VCR and the clicker and keep rewinding it. I didn't know anything about traditions because I wasn't one of those girls that grew up thinking about getting married—all that I thought about was singing."

Given her attitude toward the wedding, it was obvious that the dress would be traditional. Mariah enjoyed wearing short dresses for her videos and live shows, but get married in one? Never! It was something no bride would dream of.

The Vera Wang gown was merely one indication that no expense would be spared to make Mariah's special day perfect. The services of a top designer didn't come cheap, nor did the fabrication of a custom dress (and Wang's dresses routinely sold for $25,000). The second indication was when Mariah ordered her wedding shoes, a pair of pumps from the shoe designer Vanessa Noel, at a cost of $1000.

"Something old, something new, something borrowed, something blue." That's what they say brides should wear. Mariah had the "new" in her dress and her pumps. "Something old" was the 1893 English sixpence she planned to put inside one of her pumps. "Something borrowed" was a family heirloom, a tiara, which she had redesigned into an imitation of the one Diana had worn on her wedding day. And "something blue"? Well, it was never disclosed, but the usual thing is a garter. Whether that was the item, we don't know, but surely a bride has a right to *some* secrets, even one as visible and popular as Mariah Carey.

In the meantime, the other details were falling into place. Given Tommy Mottola's position and influence in the record industry, the guest list looked as if it was a *Who's Who* of popular music. There was at least one person invited, though, who seemed unlikely to attend: Mottola was overheard saying jokingly to Barbra Streisand, a good friend of the man concerned, that Mariah really wanted President Clinton at the church, and was there anything she could do about it? In the end, neither the Chief Executive nor his wife attended, and Mariah didn't appear too upset by their absence. But by then, she probably had quite a few other things on her mind.

IN NEW YORK City, June 5, 1993, was a rainy day. Not the type of weather a bride would choose for her big day, but the weather was one thing beyond the control of even Tommy Mottola, and the dampness certainly didn't diminish Mariah's anticipation.

Unsurprisingly, she was excited, but not too nervous at first. "The night before the wedding I didn't sleep at all," she admitted. "I hung out with my bridesmaids in a hotel suite, and we stayed up really late and had a great time. But actually, I wasn't nervous until the moment when I started walking down the aisle. I was worried that I was going to rip, or something."

Mariah might have seemed calm, but that wasn't true of the fans who gathered early to wait outside St. Thomas Episcopal Church on Fifth Avenue. It wasn't a small group who'd turned out, either; the numbers rose throughout the morning until they reached several hundred, with reporters, photographers, and television news crews jostling to the front for a better view and better pictures. This was an important occasion, a celebrity wedding, and magazines and six o'clock reports were all primed to give it coverage. But Mariah didn't find all the attention invasive.

"I mean, it wasn't annoying or anything," she said. "It was pretty exciting, actually." In terms of pictures, only one thing would sour the memory. "[O]ne of our guests had snuck in and sold a bunch of pictures when we hadn't given anybody pictures of the church or the reception. It made me feel really violated."

But that would be in the future. For now, there was still the wedding. And when Mariah arrived, she truly looked the fairy-tale bride, like Cinderella about to marry the prince. Emerging from the limousine, she was wearing a gorgeous off-the-shoulder gown in pale ivory silk, its bodice beaded over the material. The veil that covered her face was ten feet long, made of English tulle sprinkled with rhinestones to sparkle in the light and the raindrops. As she began to walk up the steps to the church doors, the dress kept coming from the car, the train slowly gathered up by six "ladies-in-waiting" until it was revealed in its full glory—all twenty-seven feet of it! "It took so many people to shove that thing in there," she laughed later. "It was . . . a major ordeal."

As major ordeals went, Mariah could have experienced much worse. In fact, things went very smoothly. The church was packed with faces familiar to any casual reader of entertainment magazines. Barbra Streisand, Michael Bolton, Bruce Springsteen (one of the few men who didn't dress in black tie) with his wife Patti Scialfa, and Robert DeNiro, for whom the event was so important he was willing to take a day's break from his directorial film debut, *A Bronx Tale.* Billy Joel and his then-spouse, supermodel Christie Brinkley; Latin pop star Gloria Estefan, fully recovered from her broken back; television sitcom star Tony Danza; actor William Baldwin, accompanied by girlfriend Chynna Phillips, formerly of the singing group Wilson Phillips; and perhaps surprisingly, heavy-metal singer Ozzy Osbourne. Even veteran disc jockey and game-show host Dick Clark was in attendance as the couple said their vows. And with the presence of such talent—all in all, there were about three hundred guests—there was quite a lot of security. In fact, security personnel numbered another two hundred.

Episcopalian services tend toward the plain and simple, not lasting too long (unlike a Catholic wedding which can stretch out for two hours), so it wasn't a tedious wait for the guests before Tommy was slipping the six-carat, pear-shaped diamond wedding ring onto the third finger of Mariah's left hand, a suitable companion for the diamond engagement ring he'd given her, which she wore on her right hand. Relatively speaking, given the size and obvious cost of the day, the ring was not ostentatious, although its worth was never stated.

Then, as the groom kissed the bride, it was over. They turned to face the photographer and video cameraman and walked down the aisle as man and wife. Outside the church, a limousine was waiting, but on the steps were the flower girls, forty-seven of them, waiting to shower the happy pair with rose petals. Then they had to run the gauntlet of fans and press before they could drive away to the reception. A whole procession of limos was soon en route to the exclusive Metropolitan Club, rented for the occasion.

The reception had the tone of a conventional wedding reception held anywhere in the country, at least unless you looked at the guests. There was a catered buffet, offering grilled shrimp, pasta, baby chickens. A disc jockey played music. Tommy had chosen oldies, songs from the Motown era and further back, including the highly appropriate "Chapel of Love" by the Dixie Cups. Mariah preferred something only a little more recent, seventies disco. When the deejay wasn't working his turntables, an orchestra was on hand to take over. Notably, none of Mariah's hits was performed, nor did any of the amazing talent on hand stand up to sing with the band.

Without any doubt at all, it was the most perfect day of Mariah's life, a bigger thrill than any number 1 ranking or Grammy award could offer. "The whole thing was like a dream," she recalled later. "Tommy has a lot of friends who happen to be famous."

Mariah and Tommy stayed for most of the reception, after which it was time to leave for their honeymoon. Like so many couples, they were going to Hawaii. Fans were still waiting, having moved from the church to the Metropolitan Club, and Mariah gave them a gift for their patience: "When I was leaving the reception it was, like one o'clock in the morning, there were a bunch of fans that had waited around. So I thought it'd be nice to throw the bouquet to them. Somebody said that I hit a guy in the head, but that's totally not true, because I saw a picture of the girl who caught the bouquet."

Inside the Metropolitan Club, the party continued, with celebrities dancing, eating, and having a chance to let their hair down together.

Later, the cost of the whole day would be estimated at $500,000. The amount could be seen as sheer indulgence, a lot of money spent unnecessarily. It could also be looked at as something both the bride and groom could easily afford without the usual scrimping and saving a wedding demands, so why not? As Mariah said, "I used to think of marriage as the end of the road; but now I'm ready to make a commitment." Commitments should be things that last; why shouldn't they—and particularly such a large one—be celebrated in style?

ON THEIR RETURN from Hawaii, the couple divided their time between two homes, an apartment in Manhattan—a necessity for both of them, but particularly for Tommy, who needed to be in the city five days a week—and an estate in Bedford, in upstate New York, located in the Hudson River valley. The house was a large, renovated colonial, expensively restored to perfect condition, with ninety acres of both woodland and mowed pasture. There Mariah could indulge her passion for the outdoors, either in vehicles—a Jeep and an ATV (all-terrain vehicle)—or on one of the four horses in the barn, including Mariah's favorite palamino, Misty.

The horses were among the new additions to Mariah's menagerie. There were still Ninja and Thompkins (as well as Mariah's oldest cat, Clarence, brought from her mother's house) and Princess, but they'd been joined by another Doberman pinscher, Duke, and Jack, a Jack Russell terrier with a passion for water.

Near the two-story main house, which stood on a hill overlooking the property and which the couple planned to expand very soon, was the guest lodge, ready for whoever might drop by.

With the peace of nature all around, it was easy to believe that this bucolic paradise was a million miles from the music business, instead of just ninety short miles from Manhattan.

Inside the main house, the decor was chic, expensive country, the two main rooms filled with comfortable couches and chairs, and saddles resting in seemingly odd places, on banisters and on the arms of chairs, ready to be carried out and used. And, of course, the place was filled with photographs of Mariah and of Tommy, and a videotape of their nuptials. Naturally, there was a copy of the wedding album—one of two, in fact; the other was in their apartment.

Their life together in the country was quite relaxed and contented. There was only one realm where Mottola was the undisputed king—the kitchen. "Tommy is a wonderful cook," Mariah said happily. "I'm *so* spoiled by his cooking. I bake when I'm bored, but he's the chef." She'd even given up her vegetarian ways—at least, to some degree—to fully enjoy her husband's cooking. And now she had that maid she'd joked about with Patricia when she was a teenager—a virtual necessity since, by her own admission, Mariah wasn't much of a homemaker, and taking care of such a place was a full-time job.

With the remodeling plans, it would be 1995 before Mariah and Tommy would truly be able to live there. The core of the house truly was old, and they wanted the rest to look the same.

"We've built it from scratch," she'd tell English *Vogue*. "I found a picture in a magazine that I liked, and we showed it to the architect, and we just built it from there. It's supposed to look like a 200-year-old, like, manor house. But it's brand new. So it was hard to make everything look old. We got the brick from Florida. Took four months to find it. It's made to look old. You can't use actual antique brick because it's too porous."

In the end, it would be a mix of styles, with domes, rotundas, colonnades, balconies, summerhouses around the grounds, even a clock tower. There would be a full recording studio where Mariah could work whenever she wanted, overlooking the indoor pool, which had the sky painted on the ceiling; there would even be a movie screening room with a chrome bar and a jukebox.

It took a long while to complete, and initially didn't do much for Tommy and Mariah's relationship with their neighbors. "Everyone is complaining," she said, "the trucks just keep going up and down." But when it was over, they had what she thought of as "a small castle." When asked how many rooms were in the house, she had to admit, "I really don't know, but since I get asked the question a lot I'll count them some day. . . . There are not *that* many actually, they are just big rooms, not so many. I need a lot of space to move."

WITH TWO STRONG people, though, both involved in the same business, there were disagreements at times, particularly since Tommy was "very creative, more than just a businessman." But their differences all seemed like nothing that couldn't be ironed out over a good meal.

Initially, people wondered when the couple might be having children, or even if they would. It was, Mariah explained, something they both wanted, but "eventually, not too soon." She still had a career ahead of her that she wanted to have time for.

IT WASN'T TOO long after the marriage, in September 1993, that Tommy Mottola received a promotion. For five years, he had headed Sony's American music division, consisting of Columbia, Epic, and associated labels. In that time, he had seen Columbia return to an ascendant position in the country, which it had lost a few years earlier to WEA (Warner Elektra Asylum). Not only had Mottola's big names (Billy Joel, Barbra Streisand, Michael Jackson) all sold very well, but under Tommy's leadership a large number of new acts had been taken on board. Some like Pearl Jam and Alice in Chains, had sold remarkably well from the beginning. Others, like the Spin Doctors, had required some development, which the label was willing to offer (although that particular band flared briefly, then died). Sony had also widened its musical net to take in hip-hop acts like Cypress Hill, whose sales proved the decision to be a wise one, and neo-folk groups like the Indigo Girls, a critically appreciated band that had come up through independent labels and ended up with large worldwide sales and sold-out concert dates around the globe.

And then, of course, there was Mottola's new wife, Mariah Carey. The sales of her two albums and the *Unplugged* EP more than justified the leap of faith Mottola had taken, not just in signing her, but in the money spent on the promotional campaign for the first record, something which had at times been criticized by people within the company. Her success was not only domestic, but global; she was popular throughout Europe, Australia, and Asia.

The jump in record sales that boosted Sony's position wasn't Mottola's only achievement within the company, however. With his background in so many areas of the music business, he helped the company rebuild its music-publishing division, a once-strong, ongoing source of income, which had been allowed to lapse. He'd also set up a joint venture with an outside entrepreneur to develop and operate outdoor concert venues. Then, in New York, the East Coast center of the industry, he'd overseen the opening of a recording and video studio with state-of-the-art equipment—Sony Studios, exclusively for Sony artists—in order to keep the whole process in-house and thereby reduce the cost of using outside studios. (It soon became the home of "MTV Unplugged.")

What all this showed was that Tommy Mottola, apart from being an astute businessman, was precisely the creative figure that Mariah had made him out to be. He had vision, and he was definitely looking to the future. Such were the requirements of the nineties executive. Being good, even very good, was no longer enough. The music industry, like every other, had become like a chess game, and to succeed, it was vital to think several moves ahead, anticipating what your rivals might do, and to be prepared to counter their moves while putting yourself in an advantageous position.

That was what Tommy Mottola had achieved. Sony was strong now, not just in record sales, but in many areas of the business. So, he had fully earned the promotion from president of Sony Music (U.S.) to president/chief operating officer of Sony Music. This moved him from a purely domestic market to a global one. He would become responsible for more than sixty markets and eleven thousand employees—which would continue to include the United States. He would, he announced, continue his policies of long-term artist development and aggressive management and marketing. What had worked in the United States should, after all, work elsewhere.

This new position rounded off a very good year for Mottola. He'd married a woman who was probably the hottest singing talent in the country, and then he'd been named to a prestigious new job. What else could happen to make it better?

Well, there was one thing. His new wife could have another hit album. Not only would he be able to be proud of her, but the bottom line on the company's balance sheet would look a whole lot better.

7

D reamlover" was the first release from Mariah's forth-
coming album, *Music Box,* her first release in over a year.
Undoubtedly, the marketing department at Columbia
was a little worried; "I'll Be There" had made number 1, but it
was an oldie, a song that had been around for more than twenty
years, familiar to many people. Of the material released from *Emotions,* only the title track had reached the top of the charts. Even if
the other releases had all managed to make the Top Five, it still
didn't have quite the same cachet. On top of that, neither *Emotions*
nor *MTV Unplugged* had managed to hit the top album spot. That
the record-buying public would be happy to hear and purchase
Mariah's new songs wasn't the question; the question was, just
how happy would they be? And as if that wasn't enough pressure,
the artist the label was now handling had just become the boss's
wife! It would be in everyone's best interest if things went
smoothly.

The way things went, the Columbia folks needn't have worried unduly. In the middle of August, the single glided onto the
charts at number 13, rising over the next couple of weeks to number 9, then to number 3, before hitting the magical number 1 on
the *Billboard* Hot 100 on September 4, 1993, Labor Day weekend,
Mariah's seventh number 1 recording. The only real surprise, and
a very joyous one, was that "Dreamlover" hogged the top spot for
a total of eight weeks, an absolute indication that, far from being
on the wane, Mariah's popularity was still increasing.

Mariah had worked on the song with Dave Hall, a record producer who'd recently finished Mary J. Blige's album. "I loved what

Dave was doing at the time," Mariah told Fred Bronson. "I wanted to do something that had a happy feeling, and that's really not Dave. It's very anti what he's about. So he said, 'Oh, you want to do that happy stuff? All right, all right.' He wasn't into doing it. Then we listened to a lot of loops, and we used the 'Blind Alley' loop and I started singing the melody over it."

The "Blind Alley" loop came from an old record, and was so low in the mix it was barely audible. "It was used on a rap record called 'Ain't No Half-Steppin' ' by Big Daddy Kane and probably a lot of other things," Mariah explained. "But it had never had this kind of a song over it. We built the song from there and I wrote the lyrics and the melody and Dave ended up liking it."

In fact, Hall ended up enjoying his entire time with Mariah.

"My experience with Mariah was a good one," he agreed. "Some artists don't arrive on time and you sit in the studio waiting. But Mariah was always on time, very on point. She's a perfectionist. She knew exactly what she wanted to do when we got in the studio. We would lay down some ideas in the morning, and she would go home with it that evening, until the next evening. We would get the hook down that night. She's pretty quick on that."

Mariah played Tommy the version of "Dreamlover" that she and Hall had concocted. While he liked it, he felt it needed more to be properly commercial, and he approached Walter about lending his talents to the track.

"Mariah and Dave did this loop thing, and it was new to us pop producers at that time," Walter said. "Their version of 'Dreamlover' was missing a lot of stuff. The spirit of the song was up but it wasn't hitting hard enough." Walter's solution was to re-arrange the drums and keyboards, to give it more swing, and more drive. "It put a whole different shade of colors to it."

As for the album itself, *Music Box* made its debut on the charts on September 17, and one week later stood poised at number 2, where it seemed to stall just shy of the top position. Indeed, it would be sometime before it gained that elusive number 1 spot—

until Christmas, to be exact, when its sales were undoubtedly boosted by copies purchased all over the country.

However, once it did achieve number 1, *Music Box* was very reluctant to move down again. It stayed there for three weeks, slipped, then came back, slipped again and returned, until it ended up spending a total of eight weeks at the peak of the chart. And while that wasn't as impressive as *Mariah Carey*'s twenty-two weeks, it remained a very welcome statistic.

Even as "Dreamlover" began to fall through the Hot 100, the next single was being prepared for release. This was "Hero," a powerful, inspirational ballad, and it was destined for another swift rise, climbing to number 1 at the same time as the album, on Christmas Day. This gave Mariah a remarkable total of eight number 1 *Billboard* singles, a feat bested by only nine artists in the entire history of the chart. Very few artists had managed more total weeks at number 1 than Mariah, either, who at this point had amassed twenty-eight. That she'd achieved all this before she was even twenty-four years old made it all the more incredible, and showed that her future in music looked not merely rosy, but positively incandescent.

Curiously, "Hero" wasn't originally intended as a song for Mariah to sing, let alone as a single. It was meant to be the theme for the movie *Hero,* starring Dustin Hoffman and Geena Davis.

"The people over at Epic Records were going to do the soundtrack for the film," Walter Afanasieff explained to Fred Bronson. "They wanted to have Mariah sing the theme to it, but they didn't really think they could because at that time you couldn't get near Mariah to do anything film-wise. So they wanted to try the next best thing, which was to have us write something."

The movie had been screened for Afanasieff, and he'd been advised that Gloria Estefan would probably sing the theme. This happened while he and Mariah were working on *Music Box.*

"I went to New York and we were in the studio and came to a break. I was sitting at the piano and told Mariah about this movie. Within two hours, we had this incredible seed for this song, 'Hero.' It was never meant for Mariah to sing. In her mind, we were writing a song for Gloria Estefan for this movie. And we went into an area that Mariah really didn't go into—in her words, it was a bit too schmaltzy or too pop ballady or too old-fashioned as far as melody and lyrics."

The two were still working on the song when Tommy came into the studio to meet Mariah. Hearing a rough take, he asked what it was, and they explained it to him.

"Are you kidding me?" he replied. "You can't give this song to this movie. This is too good, Mariah, you have to take this song. You have to do it."

And so, with some lyrical changes, making it very personal, that was what she did. Walter told the Epic soundtrack people that he'd been unable to come up with a song, and the movie's theme, "Heart of a Hero," ended up being written, recorded, and produced by Luther Vandross.

There were two versions of "Hero": "a simpler performance on tape and a more difficult one, with Mariah singing out more. But we chose a happy medium. The song really calls for not anything really fancy. But she's always fighting the forces inside of her because she's her own devil's advocate. She wants to do something that's so over the top and use her talents and the voice she has. But she also knows she has to restrain herself and do what the music really calls for."

The proceeds from the single, which stayed at number 1 for four weeks, were donated to the families of the victims of the shooting on the Long Island Rail Road, a commuter line Mariah knew well. On December 7, 1993, a man had gone on a shooting rampage on an evening train. Mariah had often taken the LIRR in her younger days, when she was still living on Long Island and working with Ben at Bedworks.

"Hero" would rapidly establish itself as a staple of MOR (middle of the road) radio, both AM and FM, to be enjoyed by all ages, as would its successor, Mariah's second-ever cover song—a sweeping, moving version of "Without You," which had been such a big, enduring hit for Harry Nilsson in the early seventies that it was generally assumed he'd written it. In actuality, it had been penned by Pete Ham and Tommy Evans of the ill-fated British band Badfinger (troubled by financial problems, both those song-writers would eventually commit suicide). They had a number of hits themselves ("Come and Get It," "Day After Day," "No Matter What," "Baby Blue"), which still receive frequent airplay on oldies stations.

But it was Nilsson's hit that Mariah had grown up with and loved, and which she used as the basis for her version. Mariah and Walter's arrangement owed a great deal to Nilsson's rendi-tion, rather than to the original, although it did strip away some of the massive orchestration that tended to overwhelm the Nils-son cut.

In a rather sad, ironic footnote, on the day Mariah's version of "Without You" was released, Harry Nilsson, only in his early fifties, died from heart problems. However, the record was not withdrawn, but allowed to stand, at least in part as a tribute to his talent (he had released a number of excellent albums, and was a very talented songwriter in his own right). "Without You" entered the Hot 100 at the end of January 1994 at number 53, then climbed speedily to numbers 35, 12, 7, then to number 6 and number 4, where it remained for three weeks before managing one more small jump to number 3, where it stayed. That would be its peak.

Even though it never reached number 1, "Without You" still enjoyed a long run on the charts, hovering in the Top Ten and never really falling until May, when the fourth single from *Music Box* was issued—another slow song, "Anytime You Need a Friend." This debuted at number 45, rising in its second week to number 32. It continued to climb until it stood at number 12 by the end of June.

Given the way Columbia had interspersed ballads and up-tempo songs as singles for Mariah in the past, it might have seemed odd that for this album they'd mostly released slower ma-terial ("Dreamlover" stood as an exception, but even that was hardly a dance tune). After all, *Music Box* did contain two collaborations between Mariah, David Cole, and Robert Clivilles, just as *Emotions* had. The logic may have been, as stated earlier, that Mariah's real strength lay with ballads, although she might have started to disagree. Certainly, within that framework, she could offer a very strong, emotional vocal, and let her voice, rather than the beat, dominate the song. "Hero" and "Without You" both offered excellent examples of that. Both used relatively simple vocal lines, but that simplicity was their real power. It was apparent from these songs that Mariah had learned a great deal about arranging a piece—as her partner, Walter Afanasieff, had learned about bringing out the best in her.

One of the first things to strike a listener to *Music Box* was that Mariah barely touched her infamous upper register. This time around, there was absolutely no reliance on that gimmick to sell her music, and in the brief instance it did occur, it provided a fitting climax to the material. Mariah was relying purely on her singing and her powers of interpretation to make the material work.

"It's not that I'm experimenting with lower notes," she told *US*. "I actually think my natural voice is low. My speaking voice is low, you know what I mean? And I'm really comfortable singing in my lower register . . . , I sing from my heart. Whatever the music makes me feel at the time, I go into the studio to sing a song, that's what it's going to do. Some people like it, some people don't. But it's just a part of my voice and that's it."

The other immediately noticeable factor was the production. As had been seen previously, Mariah was torn between two things—studio perfection and a raw, "live" sound. She loved to layer backing vocals, and her recordings used mostly synthesizers and drum machines—whereas live, she used real instruments and a large number of backup singers. On *Music Box,* it seemed as if she'd finally achieved a balance between the two apparently opposite ideals. She brought in a number of other people to sing behind her, and although she continued to make full use of synthesizers and studio technology (or, to be more precise, Walter did), there was far more space in the overall sound, letting "some air" into the songs, as it were. Everything appeared much less produced than on *Emotions*—and most definitely, much, much less produced than on *Mariah Carey,* which seemed cluttered and overflowing by comparison.

As mentioned earlier, Mariah had also expanded her circle of writing collaborators, bringing in Dave Hall for "Dreamlover," and Babyface, a star in his own right, poised on the brink of superstardom as writer, producer, and performer, for "Never Forget You." She continued to work very closely with Walter Afanasieff, with whom she cowrote six of the record's ten tracks, and with Clivilles and Cole, who were drafted to help write, perform, and produce the two dance tunes. The effect of this was to offer some stylistic variety, both in the approach to the music, and the sound of the tracks.

Music Box also seemed to have less gospel and soul influence than did its predecessors, which was a little surprising, given its overwhelming presence on *MTV Unplugged.* Where it did occur, it tended to spring from the backing vocalists, who'd all sung with Mariah before, either on *Emotions* or on *MTV Unplugged.* About the only conclusion to be drawn was that Mariah was moving forward in her music, and that, however much she loved both those styles, it was time for her to progress and change a little. For if *Emotions* had demonstrated her quick advancement from the material on *Mariah Carey,* then *Music Box* stood as a quantum leap forward.

Mariah had hinted at her growing sophistication all along, on songs like "Vanishing" and "The Wind," both of which made real use of her singing skill. But on this album, she'd fully fused that ability into every song, not only in her voice, but also in the vocal and instrumental arrangements. And while there was a danger that doing this might remove her somewhat from pop music and put her into a more adult area (which might well have been Columbia's ultimate intention), the success of the singles appeared to show that she'd been able to retain her old audience, and that the public at large had embraced this "new" Mariah with wide open arms. After all, "Hero" sold more than a million copies, and *Music Box* itself went multi-platinum. More than 6 million copies were bought in the United States alone, and over a million more in the rest of the world; these were hardly the sales figures of an artist whose popularity was fading.

ASTONISHINGLY, THE CRITICS weren't happy with this album; they seemed to find it lacking in substance and emotion. In *Time,* Christopher John Farley called it "perfunctory and almost passionless," although he did admit "there are some great moments on *Music Box.* The gospel flavored 'Anytime You Need a Friend' demonstrates Carey's vocal power, although too fleetingly. And the title cut is one of Carey's loveliest songs to date." But he felt, "One gets the sense that Carey is squandering her chance at greatness."

In *Rolling Stone,* Stephen Holden agreed that her singing had undergone "some subtle but strategic stylistic shifts" in the wake of the *MTV Unplugged* EP. But he did find that Mariah's voice had "a sustained passion that enhances the record's wedding-album feel." In the end, though, his conclusion was that the album was "precisely calculated to be a blockbuster." Even *People* found praise only for "Dreamlover," "Without You," and "Anytime You Need a Friend." Reviewer Amy Linden declared that on the other tracks, "the melodies lie limp and formless, waiting for the power of her fluid voice to give them shape."

It was, perhaps, to be expected. After the superlatives expended on the *MTV Unplugged* EP, Mariah was due for another critical backlash. It seems to stand somehow as a way of maintaining a balance of power, odd as that might sound, the reviewers' way of not letting the artists become too big and too popular. And while the critics may influence opinion to an extent, what really counts is the bottom line—how many people are willing to go and shell out those dollars they've earned for a record. In those terms, Mariah did indeed have a "blockbuster," although maybe not in quite the way the journalists had meant.

Making "Dreamlover" both the initial single and the album's leadoff track was a very sound choice. Although not typical of the album, it was a wonderful pop song, with a bouncy, breezy, summery feel—perfect for a tune released in the dog days of August. Mid-tempo, ideal for foot-tapping, it was introduced by the hook line (which would be insistently repeated throughout) played on the synthesizer. With its sample of David Porter's "Blind Alley" well hidden under the melody, the sound swirled around Walter Afanasieff's warm Hammond organ. (Porter is probably best known for his collaborations with soul singer Isaac Hayes in the sixties.) This was nothing less than high-quality pop music, which took its cues from neither soul nor gospel, but still maintained a "classic" feel over a nineties rhythm, and an atmosphere that was reminiscent of the Young Rascals' perfect summer hit of the sixties, "Groovin'." By itself, as one of her very best and poppiest compositions to date, it offered all the evidence necessary to show Mariah's growth. And if her lyrics, describing her "Dreamlover" and his qualities, were aimed at her husband . . . well, what could be wrong with that? Love could be a wonderful inspiration.

The video, directed by Diane Martel, picked up on the song's summery sheen with its images of Mariah swimming in a pool by a waterfall with her dog, Jack, lying in a field of wildflowers, and singing in front of a group of hip-hop dancers. (Mariah commented later that the water was so cold that she refused to swim until Martel dived in first.) The casual feel, almost like clips from home movies edited together, captured the song's off-the-shoulder airiness, and its frequent showing on various video-music channels did nothing to hurt the song's success.

The next track also proved to be the next single, "Hero," Mariah's most directly inspirational song yet, even more so than "Make It Happen." As she described it, "This song is saying you don't need someone to say, 'It's okay for you to do this.' If you look inside yourself, and you believe, you can be your own hero."

A lush ballad which, from its popularity in a number of radio formats, may well go on to become a standard, it made impressive use of Mariah's lower alto register. Like so many of the pieces on this album, it was very emotional, building through the verses to the chorus where both the melody and the lyrics broke through—musically, from a sad, minor key to a happier, victorious major, and lyrically, with the joy of realizing that there is a power within, whatever name one might choose to give it.

"Anytime You Need a Friend" was another pop ballad where Mariah could let her voice roam free, and interestingly, when she did so, she again kept clear of her high register, preferring a low, rough growl. Once more, there was a positive message in the words (as could be found in seven of the album's ten tracks). This song offered the only trace of gospel music on the record, and that was limited to the backing singers on the chorus; even then, it seemed muted and more secular than holy. Had this been recorded for *Emotions* or *Mariah Carey*, it would probably have sounded very different—far smoother and more fully arranged, and most certainly with more of a gospel edge, although it worked splendidly in this context.

The album's title track continued the ballads. It had a subdued, sighing, contented tone, and such a gentle love song stood tall among Mariah's compositions. It required a great deal of control to sing properly, to keep the tune's softness and sweetness without resorting to volume, and at the same time to not go too far the other way and become saccharine. Mariah managed to maintain that delicate balance in a manner that seemed effortless, floating easily above Walter's keyboards and the shimmer of Michael Landau's guitars. Lyrically, with its promise of giving and commitment, it had the feel of wedding vows, and the tinkling music-box line played on the synthesizer conveyed the sense of a wedding cake with figures of the bride and groom perched on the top.

After such a quiet piece came the record's first dance song, "Now That I Know," one of the two pieces Mariah cowrote and coproduced with the Clivilles-Cole team. After four mid- and slow-tempo songs, it offered a bright contrast, carried by the rhythm rather than the melody. Unfortunately, neither this nor "I've Been Thinking About You"—the other product of this joint effort which appeared on *Music Box*—was as strong as the dance tunes on *Emotions,* which may have been the ultimate reason neither song saw release as a single. To call them "filler" would be an exaggeration—Mariah had shown herself to be too much the perfectionist to allow such a thing—but neither was particularly memorable, a distinct disadvantage for a single. Again, the words were positive, of a woman moving from uncertainty about a lover to being sure in her own heart that love was real, which could have been taken as a reflection of her own life.

While many reviewers had taken Mariah to task for her lyrics, generally dismissing them as trite and trivial, the truth was that she had never been afraid to explore her emotions and open her heart in her songs. Never had that been more the case than on this record, where the joy was apparent throughout much of the album. Even the three sad pieces were full of compassion, however much they were tempered by sorrow. While that could have been expected from someone so deeply in love, it still remained a wonderful message to pass on, when so much that was currently being released was either full of anger and hatred (a lot of gangsta rap) or apathy (a lot of the grunge and alternative music of the period). If the mainstream artists chose to accentuate positive values like love and friendship, then all the better for them; at least, judging by their sales, they were striking a chord somewhere.

Those three sad pieces came together, beginning with "Never Forget You," Mariah's collaboration with Babyface, an R&B star with a number of hits to his credit, and his own successful label, LaFace. Another slow song, appropriately—since it lamented the loss of a love, albeit in a very tender way—it contained a lovely keyboard line that hovered over the verses. Mariah was able to indulge her passion for overdubbing her own voice for the backing vocals on the chorus. If any criticism could be leveled at the tune, it was that it slipped by too quickly. In three-quarter, or waltz, time, it had an air of partners gliding around the dance floor in memories; indeed, the very fact that it wasn't in four-four, or straight, time made it stand out, and it could quite easily have been a hit single, with an appeal that would easily have transcended generational barriers.

As has been said, Mariah's version of "Without You" owed a great deal to Harry Nilsson's 1972 hit, which had stayed at number 1 on *Billboard*'s Hot 100 for four weeks. Over the years, it had cropped up endlessly on oldies and MOR stations, to the point where it had virtually become a pop standard, with Nilsson's as the definitive version. That made Mariah's decision to cover it a formidable proposition, since Nilsson's rendition would be what her interpretation would be measured against.

There was little cause for worry. Mariah's execution was every bit as strong and tasteful as her work on "I'll Be There." From a simple piano opening, the verses remained quite stark, building to the grand swell of the chorus, where a powerful vocal was necessary to overcome the strong melody. Needless to say, that was no problem for Mariah, and the low harmony she used emphasized her head line. The backing vocalists entered close to the end of the song, adding depth and grandeur and allowing Mariah to play the diva—only one of two opportunities on the album—and to let her voice glide around the melody, once more in a low register.

Next to such a great song, "Just to Hold You Once Again" was almost bound to suffer in comparison, and in truth it wasn't Mariah's strongest writing effort. It was, however, somewhat redeemed by the use of the backing vocals, whose natural soulful tinge bolstered and added to the tune.

The song did play to Mariah's greatest strength, though—ballad singing—and by *Music Box,* that seemed to be where her real interest—or was it the interest of the record company?—lay. Lyrically, "Just to Hold You Once Again" was a despairing, confused tale, the singer still wondering why the breakup had happened, even as the love refused to leave her heart. It was only natural, with Mariah's increasing stature as an artist, that she would want to create something that would last, and with dance music becoming dated so quickly, ballads seemed like an obvious choice.

"Just to Hold You Once Again" was followed by the album's most fascinating song, the other Carey-Clivilles-Cole collaboration, "I've Been Thinking About You" (coincidentally the title of a different song, a number 1 single in 1991 for the group Londonbeat). What made it so interesting were the production tricks employed throughout the first verse, where all the instruments except percussion were dropped from the mix behind Mariah's voice, to reappear very briefly at unusual intervals, an idea adapted from reggae/dub music. It certainly had the effect of catching the listener's attention and dragging it into the song.

As a song, "I've Been Thinking About You" probably stood as the most contemporary-sounding piece Mariah had committed to tape. While much of this was due to the production (and largely the rhythm track, at that), a great deal of the arrangement ideas came from modern R&B, which in turn had taken its cues from hip-hop. So everything ended up very jerky, with no real flow, or rather the flow seemed interrupted. It was pleasant enough, but after the depth of the ballads that had preceded it, it sounded hollow, a shell without a center. One of the things that worked against it was its wordiness; merely fitting in the lines precluded the expression of emotion. How ironic, then, that out of this track Mariah would see a way ahead that would be expressed more and more over the next few years.

"All I've Ever Wanted" was the album's final track. Closing with a ballad was good, particularly one as strong as this. The song was vaguely reminiscent of Whitney Houston's gigantic international smash, "I Will Always Love You," but certainly not close enough for it to lose its own identity. And for an album that had dealt so much with love in such an honest and disarming way, this was an appropriate end. It was a simple love song quite obviously addressed to Tommy Mottola. That the melody was fairly basic was irrelevant; it was the words that were important here, echoing the sentiment of the title all the way through. It was a song that might in the future compete with Whitney's, to be sung at weddings, or at least at receptions.

Music Box as a whole had a great deal of power. It was a very personal statement, something the reviewers missed, and that may well have been the biggest piece of growth it demonstrated. Yes, musically it was more sophisticated, and often more subtle, than Mariah's earlier work. But the words pushed it across the line into art. What the critics dismissed as "hackneyed high-school poetry" really explored matters of faith—faith in love as a reason to carry on and as an inspiration. "Mostly I'm choosing specifically to write lyrics that might inspire someone, because I've been blessed with a positive and incredible life," Mariah said, adding, "I tell my stories in my own way."

Her way connected very, very well. Ten months after its release, *Music Box* still stood at number 16 on the *Billboard* album charts. It had been a top album in almost every country, from Japan to Europe to Australia. Four tracks had been released as singles, and all had been hits. The album nearly equaled—and in some ways eclipsed—the success of Mariah's debut. Nowhere near as much publicity had surrounded its release, but it still sold virtually as many copies. *Mariah Carey,* even though it contained a number of ballads, was an exuberant album, full of youth and the joy of having gotten a recording contract. *Emotions* took that one step further. There was more complexity to the songs. The slow tunes cut deeper, the gospel and soul influences stood taller. *MTV Unplugged* was a side trip in Mariah's progress in some ways, a record that portrayed her live in an ideal situation. But, looking back from the perspective of *Music Box,* it could almost be viewed as the end of an era, the culmination of those soul and gospel influences.

Allowing plenty of space in which to write, arrange, and record, and to have time to relax and breathe in the process, *Music Box* stood as the first album of Mariah's full maturity. At twenty-three, she'd already been involved in the music business for seven years, and she had seen a great deal of bad before the good arrived. She was older than her years, and that was bound to come across in her music. As she said in an interview, "I've been disillusioned a lot. . . . I think I'm constantly being let down. I'm sure I'm a giving person and a loyal person. I've tried to hold on to friends from high school, but suddenly it's 'Oh, I know her.' I'm like a topic of conversation. Since I was a kid I've always thought of myself as a hard-ass, always smart, streetwise, not vulnerable—but I am."

She'd also realized the power in what she did: "One person could say 'Hero' is a schmaltzy piece of garbage, but another person can write me a letter and say, 'I've considered committing suicide every day of my life for the last ten years until I heard that song and I realized after all I can be my own hero.' And that, that's an unexplainable feeling, like I've done something with my life, y'know? . . . It meant something to someone." And with that realization, the coyness that had sometimes marked her earlier work vanished. She was beginning to produce the work she was capable of; she had, in other words, grown into her art. This was also apparent in her singing on *Music Box*. By staying in her lower register almost the whole time, she focused attention not only on the song, but also on its power and emotive ability, rather than on all the octave tricks she could have managed. Someone with less confidence would have made more use of gimmicks.

So *Music Box* was a turning point, the start of a new musical chapter for Mariah. She'd taken stock, and she seemed to be pointing herself in a new direction. The up-tempo dance songs appeared to be there simply because they were expected—or was that all an illusion? For Mariah to have released an album composed entirely of ballads, even with a mid-paced tune like "Dreamlover," might have alienated a younger audience, and the reverse was true. For the moment, she was hedging her bets. And who was to say that she was wrong? From the sales, she apparently struck just the right note. As they say, you can't argue with success, and Mariah had certainly had plenty of that.

8

Before *Music Box* even hit the streets, Mariah's first tour had been planned. In 1992, she had said to Stephen Holden in the *New York Times,* "I'm not into performing. . . . If I toured, I wouldn't have had another album out for at least another year. It's so hard on my voice. . . . When I go out there people don't want to hear me breeze through [the songs]. They want to hear every note."

So the announcement of the venture came as something of a surprise, albeit a very pleasant and welcome one. What had changed her mind? It was never revealed, but it might well have been the enthusiastic reception her "MTV Unplugged" performance received. For someone who had once claimed such shyness, and who said she felt uneasy onstage, she'd appeared completely at home there. It might have been a controlled studio environment, but she still had to interact with and relate to the audience—a job she'd done like a pro.

It wasn't going to be an extensive tour. Quite the opposite, really. A total of just five dates were scheduled: four on the East Coast, with another outside Chicago. But that it was happening at all was enough to excite fans and to ensure that they'd be waiting in line when the tickets went on sale.

In many ways, the shows could be viewed as a way of testing the waters. Spread over a little more than a month, they offered a schedule that didn't put any strain on Mariah's voice with exhaustive travel or hotel stays. More importantly, they allowed her (and her management) to gauge just how extensive the demand was to see her live, leaving open the possibility of a longer tour in the future or, perhaps, a series of nights at selected venues around the country. Nothing was being ruled out.

"I'm jittery, but I'm very excited about it," Mariah admitted. "I didn't start out performing in clubs like most people do, so it's very new to me. I didn't want to do that, I wanted to keep it separate. I definitely wasn't ready before, although I'd done it a few times. I was thrust out into the public in front of millions of people, like when I sang at the Grammys in front of every star in the music industry. And that's crazy."

The concerts were set to happen in November and December of 1993, beginning in Miami, Florida. But well before that, the rehearsals had begun and negotiations had been successfully completed for a performance that would expose Mariah to millions, without any of them having to leave the comfort of their own homes.

Mariah's star status and the overwhelming acceptance of her MTV show had been enough to inspire someone to suggest a special on television. There was certainly plenty of precedent for it. Barbra Streisand had done several such shows in the sixties, all of which did astonishingly well in the ratings. NBC picked up on the idea, contracts were exchanged, and the wheels were set in motion.

While some might have wondered what form the special would take—would it be a variety program, with Mariah singing a few songs, then introducing guests? would there be some sort of theme?—the obvious idea was a Mariah Carey concert. Wonderful as "Unplugged" had been, it wasn't a *real* performance, in a theater. A concert format would serve two purposes: it would bring Mariah's live show to many, many people who wanted to see her but lived too far from the cities where she'd be playing on tour, and the filming would serve as a tour warm-up.

By now, Mariah had surrounded herself with a core group of top-notch musicians and singers. Most of them had worked with her on her last two albums and on the MTV appearance. They'd become used to her, and they were full of admiration, not just for her singing ability and technique, but also for her utterly professional attitude toward every aspect of her music.

These artists undoubtedly made the grinding procedure of rehearsals easier. They would also add an extra dimension to Mariah's show: a live performance would have to employ real instruments, not synthesizers and computers, and there would be real sparks created between human performers, just like on "Unplugged" but on a more elaborate scale.

There was never any doubt that Walter Afanasieff would be the musical producer of the show. He and Mariah had worked so closely for three years that they'd become almost like brother and sister. And Mariah trusted him completely. Probably only Tommy Mottola knew her better.

Essentially, the lineup that began rehearsals was the same one which had backed Mariah on MTV. Walter played piano and Hammond organ, and directed the musicians. Vernon Black was on guitar, Randy Jackson on bass, Gigi Conway on drums, and Dan Shea on keyboards. About the only changes were that Ren Klyce was now also playing keyboards, instead of percussion, and Peter Michael had replaced Sammy Figueroa as percussionist. The singers had all worked with Mariah before: Cindy Mizelle (her old friend from the days when Mariah was scuffling for session work), Deborah Cooper, Melanie Daniels, and Kelly and Shanrae Price.

Strings would be added for some of the numbers, with a base of five players who would be augmented by the Empire State Youth Orchestra. But the orchestra was extra, the icing on the television cake. The others were the ones who'd be taking the show on the road.

The program's director would be another face familiar to Mariah: Larry Jordan, or Lawrence, as he was now called. After working with her on "Unplugged" and on some of her videos, he knew full well what to look for and what to expect from her.

It was interesting that NBC chose to air Mariah's special on Thanksgiving, for it meant that the company anticipated very strong ratings for the show. The holiday is traditionally a time for families to be together, so programs with the highest ratings tend to be those which appeal to more than one sex or age group. In other words, NBC was banking on Mariah being considered vital viewing by not only the kids, but also moms and dads and grandparents. It was a sure sign that Mariah was being seen as a true entertainer, not just a pop singer.

The show was to be filmed at Proctor's Theatre, located in Schenectady, New York, an easy commute from Mariah's upstate home. An ornate, venerable building, it turned out to be an excellent location for both the set and the cameras, with a stage big enough to accommodate all the participants without seeming overcrowded. The video of the concert, rush-released in time for Christmas, captured the event in all its glory, and included extra footage of interviews with the band; Mariah and her mother; and the wrap party for the program (as well as the "Dreamlover" video).

The theater was packed with fans, mostly in their teens and early twenties. Some carried banners saying WE LOVE YOU or YOU'RE THE BEST, MARIAH. The area directly in front of the stage was crowded with those just wanting to be close, some perhaps hoping to touch their hero. This was a major event: it was Mariah's first real concert, and they were going to make the most of it.

From the audience's viewpoint, the band took up the left side of the stage. To the right stood the singers, with the string players behind them. The set, a cityscape, was simple but powerful, with plenty of lights shining both onto the stage and into the auditorium to create effects that would, at times, appear almost surreal.

Mariah's entrance was greeted with a standing ovation, a very generous gesture for her first major public show. She was dressed in her trademark black (as were all the other participants), in a long, flowing dress that was slit up both sides. Around her neck she wore the heart-shaped pendant that had made its debut in the "Love Takes Time" video, and on her left hand the huge diamond of her wedding ring caught the light.

Opening with a favorite, "Emotions," Mariah appeared relaxed and even glad to be there. The musicians swung with the beat, and the kick of a real band put an edge on her singing. Not quite as raw as Mariah's MTV show, her singing was still less polished than on her records, allowing her the freedom to weave around the lines more and to interplay with the backup vocalists, with whom she frequently traded smiles. The sound, it should be noted, was superb; everything was as clear as a studio recording.

After the rapturous reception the song drew, Mariah lowered the energy level by singing "Hero." Cameras panning across the audience showed many singing along, taking in the full meaning of the lyrics. Sung with the emotion of the moment, the song came across far more strongly in this setting than on *Music Box.* Whatever accusations had been leveled at Mariah, being a plastic performer who just mouthed the words hadn't been among them, and here she seemed to consider every line before it came out of her mouth, and to deliver it forcefully.

Notably, even live, she used her upper register very sparingly, relying, as on *Music Box,* on the quality of her voice rather than on any trickery to push her songs across.

"Hero" was followed by a costume change, with Mariah appearing next in wide flared black pants, a shiny black tee shirt, and a thin quilted vest. The new clothes brought another tempo change, accelerating the pace again with "Someday," Mariah's third number 1. The band showed their true worth here, injecting some funk under the melody and truly kicking it along, projecting the feel of a steamy dance club into Proctor's Theatre. As the crowd swayed and sang along in time, Mariah prowled from side to side like a lioness, her hair becoming more attractively tousled as she moved. She brought two of the singers out into the spotlight with her, trading voices on the choruses, a very impressive display of vocal power on the part of all three, and letting the voices build as the instruments dropped out, until the song reached its triumphant climax.

After this came another ballad, "Without You," from the newest album (this footage would also be the song's video). It was an understated version, gathering all the more strength because of it, and was a firm reminder of why Mariah had so often described her music as "vocally driven." She and the backing singers worked so well together that, with the swell of the chorus rising mightily, the instrumental accompaniment was virtually unnecessary. Even so, as on the recorded version, there was very little gospel feel to it, but rather an emphasis on the lyrics' huge sense of loss.

For "Make It Happen," her most autobiographical song, Mariah began by sitting on the edge of the stage, as hands pressed toward her and faces looked up and sang along. Even with such close personal contact, she seemed quite comfortable, as if the audience's warmth was giving her a boost. But by the first chorus, she was on her feet and moving around the stage, and things began to really loosen up.

"Dreamlover" brought the show's only color to the stage, in the form of coordinated hip-hop dancers with bright tee shirts. By this time, the strings had been cleared away, along with their chairs and music stands, leaving plenty of space. The dancers' presence at the rear of the stage, ignored by everyone else, seemed a little out of place. By her own admission, Mariah was no dancer, and no one expected to see her moving with them, but the way they were used came across almost as an afterthought, a late concession to a youthful audience. It was a shame, because they were good, although they might have been better used on a faster tune, like "Someday." (Interestingly, the choreography was by Diane Martel, who had also directed the "Dreamlover" video; obviously, she was a woman of many talents.) Still, it was more that the camera concentrated on the dancers, rather than on the dancing itself, that made them seem intrusive. Had there been some interaction between them and Mariah, however small, then they would have seemed to fit in.

But, "Dreamlover" still as bubbling and friendly as a summer's day, worked. It was one of the best pop tunes of the nineties and quite justifiably Mariah's biggest hit so far. It transformed the auditorium into a grassy meadow on an August afternoon, as people all over the theater began to smile at the song's opening notes.

Next, after the opening chords of "Love Takes Time," the spotlights dramatically caught Mariah at the rear of the stage—and *dramatic* was the ideal adjective to describe her reading of the song. With a voice full of wrenching emotion, she truly gave it everything she had. If her version of the tune on "Unplugged" had seemed low-key, this was quite the opposite. Indeed, for the rest of the show, Mariah seemed to slip into a higher gear emotionally to put her material across, and to finish on a metaphoric (if not literal) high note.

Musically, this was identical to the recorded version; what gave the song its kick was Mariah's performance. Contrasting this (and later, "Vision of Love") with the original hit, Mariah's growth over three years was quite apparent. The younger Mariah had belted the songs out, it seemed. They attacked you. The more mature woman, even with more emotion, sang with far more subtlety. She still retained the excitement, but had tempered it with experience and control, a guaranteed winning combination.

Another costume change brought Mariah back for the show's final segment. She reappeared this time in a long, tight, sleeveless black dress with a high neck, slit on the side to make movement easier.

"Anytime You Need a Friend," the fourth song performed from *Music Box,* was arranged to pay homage to Mariah's love of gospel music. The Refreshing Springs Church Choir took up the center stage behind Mariah, who perched on a stool. In their white robes, the choir members offset the other performers, and with the other five backup singers, they formed a huge wall of vocal sound, which was used to good effect. At the same time, though, it was impossible to wonder if their presence wouldn't have been better served by a song that was overtly gospelish, such as "If It's Over." However, Mariah was still able to wail over the assembled voices, and she proved that, although things might be changing, gospel still had a strong place in her heart.

"Vision of Love," the slinky song that had introduced Mariah to the world, was greeted passionately by the crowd, who seemed intent on weighing her down with bouquets of roses, offerings she gathered from their hands as she sang. There was a cocky edge to her performance. However, it wasn't dismissive of the tune—quite the opposite, Mariah treated it more like an old friend who didn't need to be handled gently. As a climax to the show, it was perfect. It had been around long enough to have been heard and recognized by a great many people. The lyrics focused on positive sentiments, on looking ahead, and its tempo was faster than much of the material Mariah had performed during the evening. But, more than anything, it left everyone wanting more, the very best thing anyone onstage can ask for.

That wasn't the last song on the video, though. That spot was reserved for an intimate version of "I'll Be There," performed on the theater's stage for a group of inner-city children sponsored by New York City's Police Athletic League, a charity with which Mariah had become involved. Mariah and the other performers were all casually dressed, and the moment captured a version of the tune that, while obviously well rehearsed, still had the spark of spontaneity. Even Trey Lorenz was on hand to sing the part he'd made justifiably famous, and Mariah's voice was an eerie imitation of a young Michael Jackson, to the point where one could close one's eyes and not be certain of the difference. The kids, of course, loved it, gazing in frank adoration at Mariah, oblivious to the cameras filming their reactions. It was a special moment, and one well worth keeping. The softness of the song let the viewer down gently, giving an appropriate end to the show.

What cannot be overstated was the importance of this program. It had been something of a test for Mariah, one she passed with honors. The filming had to have been grueling. What made it onto the screen was only a part of a long, tedious process. For every change that seemed to happen like magic, there was a great deal of work, including the laborious setting up and tearing down of microphones and chairs. In reality, Mariah did not just vanish into the wings and return a moment later in a new dress, looking fresh and glamorous. And in some ways, that made heroes of the audience, for having the stamina to wait it all out to be able to see their idol; they showed just how dedicated Mariah's fans could be.

Above all, Mariah had managed to make it an occasion. Pop concerts are a dime a dozen. You can find them in any major city almost any night of the week. So to make one stand out required something special. A performer who was rarely seen live was a good start; a performer who could really cut it live, who could offer the audience some entertainment, something that went well beyond simple, mechanical versions of the hits, was what being a star was all about.

And, quite noticeably, Mariah was relatively adventurous in her choice of material for the evening. It would have been very easy for her to have performed all her hits. As it was, she didn't even perform all her number 1 songs, leaving out the powerful "I Don't Wanna Cry." Four of the tunes came from *Music Box,* and while the album had been a big seller for almost three months, except for the hit single, a large proportion of the viewing audience couldn't have been familiar with it. Four out of ten songs was a pretty large percentage, and showed that Mariah wasn't just someone happy to sit on her laurels, but was willing to take chances.

As might have been predicted, given the direction Mariah's music was apparently taking, there was a large concentration on ballads, a further indication that they looked to be the way of the future for her.

IT MIGHT WELL have been hoped that this show would help make Mariah a face that would be immediately recognized by the American public, a star of the same magnitude as, say, Barbra Streisand. If that was the intent, then the performance hadn't been a success. While it painted Mariah's talents very clearly, she didn't show Streisand's breadth or scope. But the fact that someone who such a brief time before hadn't looked forward to being in front of an audience could come across as so pleasant and natural—almost the classic girl next door—augured well for the future. Mariah was the "nice" girl, as opposed to Madonna's engineered nastiness, and niceness was a quality with far more longevity and acceptance in the public mind. So, something was certainly achieved that night. Mariah had established her niche in the general consciousness as something more than another pop singer. The people who'd just heard her in passing on the radio could now put a face (and a smile) to the voice. And that made it a big deal.

"I was okay until I had to walk up this ramp onto the stage and I heard this deafening scream and it was kinda like everything in my life, this whole incredible whirlwind I'd been going through, it had all been leading up to that insane moment—and there I was."

MIAMI ARENA IS a huge concrete hall, not exactly the best place to hear music of any kind. The size and construction of the building obliterates any kind of subtlety. For the first night of Mariah's tour, it was almost like an enemy, designed to undermine the sound in squalls of feedback and thumping bass notes. For Mariah, it had to be something of an ordeal, a trial by fire.

The filming of the special had been fine, but this, now, was what live performance was all about: factors out of the artist's control, music that bounced back from the far wall. And, to make it worse, not all 16,000 seats had been sold. That many people would have had a dampening effect, and there would have been less reverberation. As it was, only 10,000 people turned out, mostly young couples who had brought their children along. "The audience—they knew it was my first show, they were very supportive." But Mariah was nervous. That was quite obvious from the reviews, one of which said, "Carey seemed to shrink during between-song patter. Opening night jitters led her to repeat

'Thank you' and 'I'm so happy to be here' more often than seemed natural." Still, that was hardly surprising for a performer confronted with a concrete monstrosity that attempted to stop her from hearing herself.

It was a big show that Mariah took on the road, more or less the same as had been seen on television, including the full gospel choir. For someone who was still widely perceived as a young pop star, this made it a risky venture. On television, editing cut out the time between songs, the exits for costume changes, and so on, but in the flesh they could ruin the pace of a show.

The stage set was elaborate, described by Sandra Schulman in *Billboard* as looking "oddly like an industrial church." But it was used largely as a backdrop, despite the platforms that were there. The main effect was the lighting, pinpointing the performers and also shining and sweeping into the crowd.

Needless to say, the band and backing singers were all in black, as was Mariah herself, even through all the costume changes, which had her wearing a leather jacket, then a bodysuit, and finally a gorgeous gown with a glittering necklace that she put on for the encore. As on the special, what color came onto the stage was courtesy of the choir and the dancers.

Singing, Mariah appeared quite at ease, grinning, relishing each song, and in excellent, strong voice. The times she did use her upper register brought the audience to its feet, cheering—the vocal gymnastics were evidently one of the things they'd come for.

Although she was playing to only a two-thirds capacity crowd, Mariah still gave the show everything she had. Onstage for an hour and fifteen minutes, she sang all her hits (they were, after all, her drawing card), including "I'll Be There," and added another cover song, a soul hit from the mid-eighties by the SOS Band, "Just Be Good to Me." (Interestingly, this song had been revived three years before by Beats International in a reggae version, "Dub Be Good to Me," an international hit.) She moved around the stage as if she owned it—and for seventy-five minutes, she did. Especially notable were her renditions of "Make It Happen" and "Vision of Love," where the interplay between the performers ignited and soared to create something magical, much more than the sum of its parts.

The crowd loved it, as they were meant to. In a time when an encore seems a mandatory part of any show, scripted into the set list, Mariah's was earned, and the clapping and whistling made the requests for "More" utterly genuine, particularly coming from such a sedate group.

By most standards, the night could have been termed a success, especially for a singer's first real outing. The people who'd paid to see Mariah went home happy. But with the show over, it was the critics' turn to have their say.

"Well, there were a lot of critics out to get me," Mariah said later, when the tour was well behind her. " 'This girl's sold all these albums, she's never toured, let's get her.' So they did. I turned on the TV in bed that night and the CNN guy was saying, 'The reviews are in and it's bad news for Mariah Carey.' It really hurt me a lot." The backlash had hit once again.

Happily though, although she was angry, she was still able to sort out what she saw as "valid criticism" and take it to heart, using it to make the rest of the tour better.

Billboard looked at the Miami show quite fairly. The magazine found much to praise and very little to fault in Mariah's performance. The reviewer's only advice was that "the concert seemed to be a bit too much too soon. A smaller venue with a more intimate setting would have shown off Carey's presence and ability to better advantage." Not unkind words at all.

Once she had a chance to think about it, however, Mariah realized that the reviewers hadn't necessarily been wrong, and that while the show had initially seemed good, in reality it simply hadn't been up to the standards she wanted to set. "I did a show in Florida that was *bad,*" she said later in *Vibe.* "This reviewer ripped me to shreds, and while it upset me, it helped me too. The next show, in Boston, was the best show of the tour. I let myself go more."

THAT NEXT SHOW—a week later, on November 9 at The Centrum in Worcester, Massachusetts, near Boston—showed that Mariah really had listened, and had fine-tuned her performance as a result. A sellout crowd of 11,046 watched her weave her magic out of thin air—all managed, she said, because "I took all the anger and put it out there in my next show." It certainly helped that it was one of those perfect nights musicians occasionally have, where everything clicks, and it's impossible to do any wrong. After the opening act—the up-and-coming folk duo The Story—had warmed up the audience, Mariah appeared, beaming, striding across the stage, truly singing her heart out in front of a band that didn't just get behind the beat, but kicked it along. Whatever jitters she'd felt in Miami had been exorcised; if she'd seemed in good voice there, in New England she'd never sung better. The material was the same as the last show, but seemed fresh, as if the performers were a hungry young group, still scratching around and looking for its big break, rather than seasoned, precise professionals.

The audience was with Mariah from even before the first note. And as the evening progressed and they were caught up in her spell, it was impossible for them not to know something remarkable was going on while they watched. She didn't have to win them over, they were already hers, but she did it anyway, taking the time to chat with them between numbers, coming across as personable, relaxed, and confident.

It was certainly enough to make a believer out of the *Boston Globe*'s critic, who admitted he'd been a skeptic before the show. The review he turned in was nothing short of an unqualified rave, praising "a spectacular performance . . . [which] bowled over the crowd with a confidence that grew before their very eyes." If Mariah had harbored any doubts about her ability to put on a live show that did justice to her talents (and after Miami, she might have had some), those words would have convinced her that she could do it. The tour, which she agreed to, in part "to give something back to the fans," was giving them an unexpected bonus—a glimpse of Mariah Carey as a towering live performer.

If one single moment can ever be seen as a turning point, that night at the Centrum was it for Mariah. She moved to a new level with her performance, and achieved something even she might not have been aware she was capable of doing. And with it came the realization that she could do it again, and that she would *want* to recapture that incredible feeling. It was a new goal to strive for—no bad thing, since she'd already managed to achieve all her other goals. And it most definitely closed the door on any talk that Mariah was simply a studio artist or any kind of manufactured star. She could stand very well on her own two feet, thank you.

And she knew just how she'd managed it. "[I] let go my inhibitions and just lost myself in performing." The rest—the applause, the praise—all flowed out of that.

It's a testament to Mariah that she was able to maintain the level of intensity for the remaining tour dates. Granted, there were only three of them, but magic is a difficult thing to conjure out of the blue. Performing on a high level night after night when you also have to find time to sleep, eat, and travel is virtually a superhuman task. So it probably helped that there was time between shows for her to regroup, and that the final show, at New York's Madison Square Garden, would more or less be a homecoming for the Long Island girl.

Nonetheless, Mariah's show was something that went beyond the usual level of professionalism. Someone paying upward of $22.50 (the cheapest ticket on the tour—the highest was $37.50) had a right to see a professional performance. What most of the thousands who came out to see Mariah got was something far greater.

After Worcester, there was an eight-day break before a show on November 17 at Rosemont Horizon in Rosemont, Illinois, outside Chicago. Once more, it was a sellout, with 9,438 fans crammed into the theater. The time gap between gigs allowed the stage set to be hauled from New England to the Midwest. It also allowed the performers a chance to go home to their families, rest, and recharge their batteries—most particularly Mariah, who, much as she enjoyed traveling, had no love of hotels, where it was difficult to sleep, or their canned air, which affected her throat. And she was still enough of a newlywed not to want to be away from her husband a moment longer than necessary.

The group Theory opened the Rosemont show, but it was Mariah people were waiting to see. Naturally, as she took the stage, there was a gigantic eruption of applause and cheers. It had already become the norm, but such a welcome was still an enormous rush for Mariah. It told her that the audience was with her every step of the way, rooting for her.

The set list—the songs to be performed—duplicated all the previous shows. Once again, Mariah managed to find that kick of energy, that spark to ignite the evening and make it into something very memorable for those in attendance. None of the practicalities had changed since Miami. There were still the costume changes, the gospel choir, the dancers. But New England had effected a change in everyone. The music now had an edge. The dance tunes bounced more and got everyone moving. The ballads were sadder, more desperate. And yet again, the critics were convinced that Mariah was more than a pop-chart confection.

THEN THERE WAS a two-week break over Thanksgiving. Of course, during that time, Mariah's television special was aired on NBC, giving her a larger audience than any crowd she could draw into a theater. When the crew returned to the road, it was for a short journey from New York to Philadelphia, and a date on the second of December.

Without any doubt, there was a warm atmosphere to this show, for Mariah's good friend and protégé, Trey Lorenz, was the opening act. His album had done well, as had the single from it—more than enough to be very encouraging for the future—and this date would show that he too was a force to be considered as a live performer.

The show was a sellout. Over 12,000 people filled the Spectrum to see Mariah. For many of them, Trey's set was a bonus; his music was like Mariah's, and he was a sweet singer with a gentle personality. It was all very nice, but he wasn't Mariah, and polite as the audience was, they'd paid $25 and up to see the real thing.

Which they did. Once more, Mariah charmed them with her naturalness, amazed them with her voice and her songs, and kept the real world at bay for a while. She created a cocoon, a little place for everybody in the hall, a spun shell of notes. Magic.

THE FINAL, FIFTH show came eight days later, on December 10, at New York's Madison Square Garden. It was a hometown show. After all, Mariah was a born-and-raised New Yorker: she knew these people, if not individually, then by attitude, by history. She could relate to them all quite easily.

But there was also a downside to being a hometown girl. She would be looked at more closely. The reviewers would be sharpening their knives. And everyone would expect more from her, special treatment. Not only was it her hometown, it was New York, where every performer was supposed to give something extra. And it was the last date of the tour.

It was by far the biggest concert of her career. Philadelphia had brought out 12,000, quite a crowd, but the Garden held 15,627. There were plenty of towns in the country smaller than that.

As it turned out, Mariah didn't quite manage to sell out the place. Taking up 96 percent of the building's capacity, 15,050 people paid from $28.50 to $37.50 to spend an evening with her—very respectable, when long-established acts often sold far fewer tickets.

So Mariah went into the show with something to prove. She'd

managed to wow them elsewhere; now it was the Big Apple's turn. If the reviewers carped because she was playing arenas and stadiums on her first tour, well, she'd show them why.

What she gave them was what she'd given Miami, Boston, Chicago, and Philly—herself, every little bit, singing her heart out—enough to impress Jon Pareles in *The New York Times,* who noted, "Beyond any doubt, Ms. Carey's voice is no studio concoction. . . . [R]ock concerts aren't known for precise intonation, she sang with startling exact pitch." His description of the show as "triumphant" was a high accolade from such a respected newspaper, which wasn't prone to giving such praise lightly.

For "Just Be Good to Me," Mariah wore a black leather cap of the type associated with seventies discos. When the song ended, she took the cap from her head and tried to fling it into the audience. Unfortunately, it somehow ended up behind her, which amused not only the crowd, but cracked up everyone onstage—including Mariah. She picked the cap up, commented on how weak a future she had in professional sports, and tried again. This time she succeeded, and the people loved it. It made her one of them, human and fallible; the only difference was that she'd made it, and it made them realize that they could, too.

On a more somber note, the concert came just a few days after the tragic shootings on the Long Island Rail Road. Mariah had already announced that the profits from "Hero" would be donated to a fund set up to help the victims' families. Now she dedicated the song to those victims.

But the concert couldn't end in such a serious vein. She needed to lighten up, and for a final number, that was exactly what she did. It was December, Christmas was in the air, and Mariah wasn't going to let anyone forget it. "I was going to sing 'Santa Claus Is Coming to Town.' I had a red dress, a sort of Jessica Rabbit dress. And I had five people backstage, and they couldn't zip it up. The band was vamping the intro. Four times. The crowd was yelling. And I'm behind a tiny little curtain with five people going, 'You guys better get that up! Right now! Do it, you guys!' And though it's not totally my personality, I became, like, the world's biggest bitch. Meanwhile [fake] snow was falling and the band is vamping and the crowd is screaming and finally they say, 'You better go right now, Mariah!' So I said, 'I hate all of you,' and I ran out. I'm out there singing, waving my arms and everything, in this sexy, low-cut dress and I made it through."

And so the tour ended. Her "flamboyance was just right" for large stages. She proved to the world at large that she was a very strong live performer. While the tour might not have satisfied everyone—there were still too many parts of the country she hadn't played—at least they had the consolation of the television special. Mariah's career had advanced by stages, and she'd conquered another one. The question was, what next?

9

What next? For the moment, the answer seemed to be: very little. "Dreamlover" was nominated for a Grammy, but surprisingly, it didn't win, although its obvious popularity helped make up for the loss (as a single, it sold more than a million copies). *Music Box,* oddly, wasn't even nominated. However, it would become Mariah's best-selling record to date, shifting a staggering 20 million copies worldwide.

As 1994 progressed, it became apparent that Mariah was finally taking time for herself. "Anytime You Need a Friend" peaked at number 12, and no further singles were released from the album. But for fully three-quarters of the year, *Music Box* remained on the Top 100 of the *Billboard* album charts.

However, Mariah couldn't stay away from the singles chart for too long. She returned, accompanying Luther Vandross in a duet, a remake of the song "Endless Love," which had been such a huge hit for Diana Ross and Lionel Richie in 1981, when it sold more than 2 million copies. This version, which was taken from Vandross's album, was produced by Walter Afanasieff, which provided the connection between the two singers (as did the record label, with Vandross also appearing on Columbia).

By the end of October 1994, "Endless Love" had reached its highest point, number 3 on the Hot 100. But by then, there was word of a new Mariah Carey album, which had remained a well-kept secret until the middle of the month, when it was announced in *Billboard.*

A Christmas album might have seemed an odd choice for a woman who'd become the best-selling female artist of the nineties, but to Mariah it made perfect sense. "I'm a very festive person and I love the holidays," she explained. "I've sung Christmas songs since I was a little girl. I used to go Christmas caroling."

She'd actually begun recording the album just after Christmas the year before. "The first song I did was 'Silent Night.' The decorations didn't seem too out of place in the room at that point, and it didn't seem too strange to be singing Christmas music." As time passed, and the seasons turned into spring and summer, it became "kind of like the Christmas that never ended," with decorations still hanging in the studio for atmosphere.

The album, entitled simply *Merry Christmas,* appeared in record stores on November 1, heralded by a full-page advertisement in the Sunday *New York Times.* The timing was obviously perfect for the Christmas market, and showed that Columbia was pitching Mariah as an entertainer, rather than limiting her to the pop market. But even so, there would be subtle differences for different markets. Mariah's "All I Want for Christmas Is You" would go to the Top 40 and to Adult Contemporary charts. "Miss You Most (at Christmas Time)," also written by Mariah, would be sent to R&B radio, while "Born on This Day," which Walter and Mariah had cocomposed, would be the track serviced to Christian and gospel radio. Videos had been completed for the first two (the video for "All I Want for Christmas Is You" had actually been shot the Christmas before).

As if that wasn't enough, there would be several club remixes of "Joy to the World," to ensure that *everyone* would be spending Christmas with Mariah. If it seemed calculated, it was worth remembering that Mariah's audience truly was everywhere. And this album, ranging from traditional music to pop to gospel, offered something for each of them.

Recorded at Sony Studios and the Hit Factory in New York, *Merry Christmas* used many of the musicians who'd worked with Mariah in the past. Needless to say, Walter Afanasieff played a major role, coproducing and co-arranging the majority of the record's ten tracks, and playing keyboards. But Melanie Daniels,

Shanrae Price, and Kelly Price also returned to sing background vocals. And there was also Loris Holland, whom Mariah asked in. "He co-arranged and coproduced some of the songs," she said, "and that added a really authentic gospel flavor to a lot of the stuff."

Finally, in this setting, Mariah had been able to record some real gospel music. Her version of "Silent Night" had large elements of the style, but it was on the final track, "Jesus, Oh What a Wonderful Child," a traditional song, that things really took flight. "We cut the track live and had the guys that play it in church and the girls singing it. I had all my backup singers and their husbands and their babies playing tambourines, so we got to experience some real authentic church flavor."

The song really did sound as if it had been recorded in church, with a simple combo (keyboards, bass guitar, drums, percussion, backing vocals, and Mariah) cutting loose. Mariah's love of gospel really came through here; she led the band without pushing herself forward, letting the song develop and work out, trading lines with the chorus until, after the crescendo, the musicians moved into a fast double time to the end. As a finale to the album, it was perfect—pertinent to the season, religious without being offensively so. And it left the listener wondering whether Mariah would someday fulfill her promise and record an entire gospel album.

The cover songs on the album were all familiar. Mariah's rendition of "Santa Clause Is Comin' to Town," the song she'd sung at Madison Square Garden, wasn't as rock-and-roll as the version Bruce Springsteen and the E Street Band released in 1981, but it was still sprightly and appealing. Hoyt Axton's "Joy to the World," which had been a number 1 hit for Three Dog Night in 1971, was joined to the traditional song of the same name to create something far less secular.

Mariah had never hidden her feelings about (and her gratitude to) God, although she'd never pushed them on her audience. But the reverence in her heart was allowed to shine through in a gentle way on *Merry Christmas*. Half of the ten songs were religious, and quite unashamedly so, which was certainly appropriate and perhaps even praiseworthy, given the way commerciality had overtaken the season.

There was no danger of the album becoming too serious, though, with tracks like "Santa Claus Is Comin' to Town" and a playful cover of "Christmas (Baby Please Come Home)." The latter, written by the Spector-Barry-Greenwich team, first saw light on Phil Spector's *Christmas Album* in 1963, when it was sung by Darlene Love. Mariah obviously loved the song, and while she and Walter didn't try to reproduce Spector's trademark "wall of sound" technique, they did have fun with the style.

Merry Christmas also contained three new Carey-Afanasieff compositions. "All I Want for Christmas Is You," "Miss You Most (At Christmas Time)," and "Jesus Born on This Day." The first was up-tempo, a love song that could quite easily have been written for Tommy Mottola, full of images of the Christmas magic that was all too often lost after childhood.

"Miss You Most (at Christmas Time)" was a sad ballad, very much in line with the work Mariah had produced in the past, the type of tune that had provided most of her hits. Over keyboards and a synthesized orchestra, courtesy of Walter, Mariah sang of a long-gone lover, crystallizing the way that Christmas brought memories of the past into focus.

But of the new songs, it was "Jesus Born on This Day" that was the most surprising. A full-blown production number, it employed not only Walter's synthesized orchestra, but background singers and a children's choir as well. The tune was quite solemn and hymnlike, but the arrangement, oddly, made it less religious and rather more glitzy, behind lyrics that overtly praised Jesus.

As Mariah told Larry Flick in *CD Review,* "You have to have a nice balance between standard Christian hymns and fun songs. It was definitely a priority for me to write at least a few new songs, but for the most part people really want to hear the standards at Christmas, no matter how good a new song is."

Merry Christmas certainly appeared set to do well in its first year, entering the *Billboard* chart at number 30 within two weeks of its release. The video for "All I Want for Christmas Is You," with Mariah romping in the previous winter's snow, was premiered on MTV with much hoopla on November 28.

But the star on the tree came on December 14, with the "Mariah Carey Christmas Special" on MTV. In conjunction with the release of the album, the music video channel had run a contest that offered the prize of a trip to New York, $10,000, and a chance to meet Mariah and attend her December 8 concert to benefit the Fresh Air Fund.

The one-hour special featured extensive footage of the winner, and showed her spending some of her winnings. It also included the alternative video for "All I Want for Christmas Is You," presented in a black-and-white sixties style, with go-go dancers, backup singers, and Mariah herself, in a minidress, white boots, and teased-up hair, looking for all the world like a member of the Ronettes.

The show climaxed with an out-and-out gospel performance of "Joy to the World" from the Fresh Air benefit show. Helping underprivileged children had long been close to Mariah's heart, and the benefit, which combined this impulse with her singing, was a truly bighearted gesture. With *Merry Christmas* climbing rapidly all the way to number 3, it made a perfect cap for the year.

But that was far from the end of the story for the record. Every subsequent Christmas, it would be rereleased, and by early 1998, it had sold 8 million copies—a phenomenal number for a seasonal album.

EVEN AS *Merry Christmas* reached the stores, Mariah was looking ahead to her next "real" record. "I already have seven songs," she told Craig Rosen in *Billboard*. "I don't know when it's going to come out, but I want to go into the studio soon and start recording. I don't really stop writing and stop having musical ideas. I like to keep everything flowing."

But the album was still in the formative stages. There was plenty to keep Mariah occupied, not the least of which had been the Fresh Air Fund benefit concert at St. John the Divine, a Manhattan cathedral.

The Fresh Air Fund was dedicated to taking underprivileged kids from New York to summer camp in the country, exposing them to another world. "I had gone to a camp when I was little," Mariah recalled in a radio interview, "it was . . . an underprivileged kids' camp and I hated it. It was . . . the worst experience of my life, so I thought that I could contribute to making something not so horrific as that for those kids. So they happened to have a camp that needed someone to . . . get behind it and help with the finances and things."

Her concert did more than just raise a little money for the camp, a Career Awareness Camp in Fishkill, New York—it completely funded it, bringing in $700,000.

And that was enough, in July 1995, to have it renamed Camp Mariah. "It's amazingly flattering to me of course," she said, "but it dictates to me that I should do even more. . . . I want to teach the kids about the recording business and show them they can be singers, engineers, record company presidents or secretaries."

Mariah had also become involved in other charity work, primarily with the Police Athletic League in Manhattan. In one instance, combining good works with her love of fashion, she attended a Chanel show and luncheon to benefit the obstetrics department of New York Hospital–Cornell Medical Center. While no one would have doubted that such things were in her heart, she did say, "I try to be a good person and make a difference where I can, in the world and with people."

Her involvement with the Fresh Air Fund had sprung from childhood memories, but a family event proved to be the catalyst. Mariah's sister, Alison, had been diagnosed as HIV positive. She'd been addicted to drugs and worked as a prostitute, although she was the mother of a son.

"When I found out she had AIDS I cried for days," Mariah recounted in *Bravo*. "She could never really care for her son again. He now lives with my mother [during 1995, this would lead to claims of kidnapping from Alison, which divided the family]. This sad family story made me care more about other children in need. To give them advice and to see that they get a better life. I think organizations like the Fresh Air Fund are really important because some kids just don't have a role model in their lives, someone they can get comfort from, to point out the right direction in their lives."

No CHRISTMAS WOULD have been complete without gifts, and that year Mariah had bought the ultimate gift for Patricia Carey, the kind of thank-you she'd always wanted to give—a new house.

Patricia was still living out on Long Island, and with Mariah spending most of her time up in Bedford, it was hard for them to see each other. Mariah's solution was to move her mother closer, and she planned the whole thing as a complete surprise.

"I said, 'I want to get a house for you, but right now there's nothing on the market.' So, I made up the whole lie," she recounted in an interview with Jamie Foster Brown. "It was almost a year ago. So I said, 'What we can do is take some of your stuff out of the house and put it in storage, because when you move, it'll probably be January or February and there won't be any time.' I said, 'It'll be too much snow on the ground to get the piano and all that kind of stuff.' So she thought there was something going on, but when I sent the people over there, I had them write out a slip and make like it was going to storage."

Then Mariah took some time and decorated the house she'd secretly bought for Patricia. "I put everything in there down to her food and pajamas. I got all her old pictures of her and her mom and framed them and put them on a wall." The furniture— all picked out by Mariah—was new, but she knew her mother's tastes.

Finally, Mariah was ready to present the house to her mother.

She installed two friends, Ronnie and Carol, in the house, making it seem as if it were theirs. Then she told her mother the friends were coming along to help them look at properties, but they'd have to go and pick them up first.

Mariah pulled into the driveway of the rustic, secluded place, and her mother was enchanted. "Carol was standing in the door. She said, 'Come on in, Pat.' And we walked in and she was looking around and saying, 'Wow, this is gorgeous!' So all of a sudden, I point up to the wall and I go, 'Mom, look.' It was her pictures and everything, and she almost fainted. . . . It was the most incredible thing I've ever been able to do."

10

Mariah might have started 1995 with several songs, but it would be another nine months before her fans got to hear them. The first thing they heard, at the end of September, was "Fantasy." If "Dreamlover" had seemed like a great single, this one was even better, with a slinky hip-hop groove, a sensuous vocal, and the kind of hook that just sank into the brain.

It was as close to absolutely perfect pop as Mariah had come. That seemed to be the overwhelming opinion all across the United States. On its release, "Fantasy" did what only one other single (Michael Jackson's "You Are Not Alone") had ever done before: it entered the *Billboard* Hot 100 at number 1. This made Mariah the first woman ever to accomplish this, and it meant that "Fantasy" was playing almost everywhere during the fall, as it stayed in the top position for eight straight weeks.

The single was coproduced with Dave Hall (who'd worked with Mariah on "Dreamlover"). "I had the melody idea for 'Fantasy' and then I was listening to the radio and I heard 'Genius of Love' [the 1982 hit for the Tom Tom Club, a side project for members of Talking Heads], and I hadn't heard it in a long time," Mariah told Fred Bronson. "It reminded me of growing up and listening to the radio and the feeling that song gave me seemed to go along with the melody and the basic idea I had for 'Fantasy.' I initially told Dave Hall about the idea and we did it."

Once the idea had clicked into place, and permission had been gained from the Tom Tom Club to sample the song, putting everything together was a snap.

"Mariah brought me 'Genius of Love' and I laid some strings

on it," Dave Hall recalled, "and put it to a groove that I felt would really fit her. And that song didn't take us but a minute to do, because she really busted that out within two days. We did a rough copy and let Tommy Mottola hear it and he loved it, so all we had to do was bring it back in and mix it down."

The song itself made a huge splash, but what went one better was the remix that was included on the single, by Sean ("Puffy") Combs, with a rap by O.D.B. (Ol' Dirty Bastard) of the Wu-Tang Clan. This giant step toward hip-hop was going to get noticed, although Mariah insisted that she'd "always been a fan of hip-hop music," and having grown up in New York, it was likely she had been.

The choice to use Puffy, who wasn't widely known outside hip-hop circles then, seemed odd; Mariah could have had her pick of any name producer to do the remix. "He's so known in the street and he's one of the best people out there. . . . We kind of did what we both do and having O.D.B. took it to another level. He was my ultimate choice, so I was really happy about the way it turned out."

If Puffy had seemed like an odd selection, O.D.B. was just plain weird. No one had thought of a collaboration between Mariah and Wu-Tang. "I've been a fan of his style since Wu-Tang first came out," she said. "I just think it's kind of unique about how he raps and kind of sings, too. I thought that because we were using the Tom Tom Club track that his voice was perfectly suited for it. We got a hold of him, and we did it. He basically went in and freestyled."

Even with this first single, it was obvious that Mariah had been very involved. She'd even directed the video for "Fantasy," which premiered September 7 on the MTV Music Video Awards. Set in one of Mariah's very favorite places, an amusement park—the same old park where scenes from *Big* and *Fatal Attraction* were shot—it showed Mariah roller-blading, the odd image of a clown tied to a pole, and Mariah singing along on a roller-coaster ride. "They did not expect me to get that shot!" she admitted. "They were saying, 'How's she going to sing on a roller coaster?' . . . We put a little speaker in the bottom of the car, where my feet were. We built the rig in front of the roller coaster and the lens kept falling off!"

Directing seemed a natural extension to Mariah, given that she'd been unhappy with some of the results in the past. "I just wanted to do it because it's . . . it's my song and I really want it to come out the way I want it to be."

For a debut, it was very impressive, as professional as any other video out there. Taken all together, the pieces seemed to indicate that this was a new Mariah, taking herself and her music to new places, very much in control of what she was doing.

Certainly, she was projecting herself at new markets. Before *Daydream,* as the album would be called, was released in the United States on October 3, it would be issued overseas. Mariah flew to London to publicize "Fantasy" there with an appearance on "Top of the Pops," a British television chart show, as well as a live performance, via satellite, for Asian television. There was even talk of a world tour in 1996!

WITH THE PERFORMANCE of "Fantasy," it was no surprise to anyone that *Daydream* went straight into the *Billboard* album chart at number 1. The single had gained Mariah a lot of new fans, and after all, *Music Box* had ended up selling a staggering 23 million copies worldwide. *Daydream* couldn't quite match that, but it did manage to sell 9 million copies in the United States alone, with close to 20 million around the globe, and it spent three weeks in the number 1 position.

The new record showed a somewhat different Mariah, one who seemed to be distancing herself from the image created by *Music Box.* That album had been heavy on the ballads, which were still there on *Daydream,* but not to the same extent. Instead, there was a leaner sound, a good deal of which seemed weighted toward R&B. "Fantasy" scored there, but so did "One Sweet Day,"

Mariah's collaboration with Boyz II Men; "Always Be My Baby," which teamed her with well-known hip-hop producer Jermaine Dupri; "Daydream Interlude (Fantasy Sweet Dub Mix)," which she coproduced with club guru David Morales; and "Melt Away," a collaboration with the amazingly successful Babyface, a track Mariah produced herself. There was even another cover, this time of Journey's "Open Arms," which, she said, "was my idea. For years I have been a fan of [Journey singer] Steve Perry. He has a fantastic voice. I have been singing his songs since my youth! I already have sung a lot of covers, but I keep enjoying it. I used to love singing along with the songs I heard on the radio. The version of 'Open Arms' is my own interpretation."

For the slower material, Mariah had again collaborated with Walter Afanasieff, both in the studio, behind the boards, and writing. But even the ballads were more sinewy than before, the arrangements stripped down, particularly on "Looking In," where Mariah seemed to reflect on her life and career so far. "It is a very personal song," she agreed, "but it is more about a mood. We all go through different moods, you can't always feel happy—it's showing a different side. When you are in the public eye, people seem to think they know all about you—they form a perception which often bears little relation to the person."

After "Fantasy" had been number 1 for two months, it was replaced by Whitney Houston's "Exhale (Shoop, Shoop)," from the *Waiting to Exhale* soundtrack. But it only stayed there for one week, as the second single from *Daydream* did something unheard of— it became Mariah's second single in a row to enter the *Billboard* Hot 100 at number 1, a feat unequaled by any other artist.

"One Sweet Day" teamed Mariah up with Boyz II Men, an irresistible combination of two of the hottest talents in music. "I wrote the initial idea for 'One Sweet Day' with Walter," she explained, "and I had the chorus. . . . I stopped and said, 'I really wanna do this with Boyz II Men,' because . . . obviously I'm a big fan of theirs and I just thought that the work was crying out for them, the vocals that they do, so I put it away and said, 'Who knows if this could ever happen, but I just don't wanna finish this song because I want it to be our song if we ever do it together.' "

For Mariah, whose good friend David Cole, the man who'd worked with her on two albums and "MTV Unplugged," had recently died, the song was about the "whole idea of when you lose people that are close to you, it changes your life and changes your perspective."

Finally, she had the chance to team up with Boyz II Men. "When they came into the studio I played them the idea for the song and when [it] finished, they looked at each other, a bit stunned, and told me that Nat [Nathan Morris] had written a song for his road manager who had passed away. It had basically the same lyrics and fitted over the same chord changes."

Was it coincidence, or just meant to be? "It was really, really weird," Mariah said. "We finished the song right then and there."

"We were kind of flipped about it ourselves," Shawn Stockman agreed. "Fate had a lot to do with that. I know some people won't believe it, but we wouldn't make up such a crazy story."

The recording session itself was the video, and that meant, as Walter Afanasieff recalled for Fred Bronson:

> It was crazy! They had film crews and video guys. I'm at the board trying to produce. [Boyz II Men] are the busiest guys in the world. Their managers and bodyguards are in the waiting room and it's 4:30 and they have until 7 o'clock. You've got four guys and you haven't even worked out their parts yet. So I was sweating. And these guys are running around having a ball, because Mariah and them are laughing and screaming and they're being interviewed. And I'm tapping people on the shoulder. "We've got to get to the microphone!" They're gone in a couple of hours, so I recorded everything they did, praying that it was enough. After going home to my studio, I put the tracks together and did a rough blend of the four guys. And then Mariah went in and did some more voices to

fill in a little bit, because it sounded like it's all Boyz II Men and there wasn't enough Mariah Carey on it.

But it wasn't enough for "One Sweet Day" to break one record. With that combination of talent, and that song, it just kept on selling and selling, keeping its number 1 position against all comers. Previously, the longest any song had stayed there was fourteen weeks (a three-way tie between Whitney Houston, Boyz II Men, and Los Del Rio), but "One Sweet Day" cruised past them all, ending up with an amazing sixteen weeks there, and giving Mariah yet another record to add to her collection.

"One Sweet Day" was eventually replaced by Celine Dion's "Because You Loved Me," but Mariah wasn't finished with the singles chart yet. On May 4, 1996, "Always Be My Baby" toppled Dion's single. It hadn't gone straight in at number 1, but it did manage to climb there, giving Mariah her eleventh number 1 hit (which put her in a tie with Whitney Houston and Madonna as the female artist with the most top singles). And, as with "Fantasy," there was a hip-hop remix, featuring a rap by Da Brat, with a video shot at Camp Mariah.

Mariah had been a fan of musician and producer Jermaine Dupri ever since she'd heard Kriss Kross's "Jump" (Dupri had gone on from there to found his own So So Def label). For "Always Be My Baby," Mariah noted, "Jermaine, Manuel [Seal] and I sat down and Jermaine programmed the drums. I told him the feel that I wanted and Manuel put his hands on the keyboards and I started singing the melody. We went back and forth with the bridge and the B-section. I had the outline of the lyrics and started singing 'Always be my baby' off the top of my head."

Although the background vocals included her longtime cohorts Kelly and Shanrae Price and Melonie (formerly Melanie) Daniels, it was mostly Mariah, building the wall of voices that she loved. This would be true for all the album's backing vocals.

This time out, there was no long stay at number 1, but that

didn't matter. The singles from *Daydream* had given Mariah more than six months at the top, something virtually unbelievable in the modern age.

Overall, *Daydream* won over the critics, even those who'd been harsh in the past. In *People,* David Hilbrand called it her "best album," and noted that *"Daydream* vaults over its pop predecessors because the material is both funkier and mellower. Carey also has better control of her instrument—her voice evincing greater muscularity and agility." He concluded that the remarkable thing about the record was that "Mariah makes it all sound so effortless."

Entertainment Weekly's Ken Tucker found the ballads "grandiose," but found plenty to enjoy in "One Sweet Day," "Always Be My Baby," and "Forever." To him, however, it was "Daydream Interlude (Fantasy Sweet Dub Mix)" where "the singer really defines herself. At her best, as she is on this clipped, spunky track, Carey is a disco diva for the '90s, a worthy successor to women like Donna Summer and Vicki Sue Robinson, R&B singers with an affinity for the endless groove."

And the *New York Times* reviewer felt that Mariah's "songwriting has taken a leap forward, becoming more relaxed, sexier, and less reliant on thudding clichés," and called *Daydream* "subtly innovative." It was obvious, the review stated, that Mariah was "struggling to develop a more personal lyrical voice. Whether or not she succeeds almost doesn't matter so long as she continues to make pop music as deliciously enticing as the best moments of 'Fantasy.' "

So Mariah finally had what she'd been striving for for five years—respect. The public loved her, but it had taken a long time for the critics to come around to her side. But, in truth, this was her best album yet, the sound of someone who was finding herself, asserting her own identity.

"Fantasy," with that nagging Tom Tom Club sample, led things off on a very high note indeed, a breezy, catchy piece of pop music that worked off a groove as much as a melody, with Dave Hall providing all the instruments and programming. While it harked back to the eighties, there was still a completely contemporary feel to it.

"Underneath the Stars," which followed, was the first track recorded for the album, and it "has a real '70s soul vibe," Mariah thought. "We even put those scratches you hear on old records to give it that kind of flavor. [It] was a good place to start, because it got me into the head of making an album that was more R&B—more in the vibe of the Minnie Ripperton era, which has always been an inspiration to me." And indeed, it had that feel, melodic and airy. But unlike Minnie's recordings, there was little evidence of Mariah's higher register. Indeed, as she'd progressed from *Mariah Carey,* she'd used it less and less. As she explained to Tabitha Soren on MTV, "[W]hat I tried to do is put it, sort of, as more of a texture on a lot of songs, like as a background part I did certain things, and you know I just meant to get a little bit more creative with it." Which was exactly what she'd done. Her reputation and following were strong enough now that any gimmicks were unnecessary.

"One Sweet Day," along with "Fantasy," was the song most people knew from the album, and with its run at number 1, it was almost impossible not to have heard it. But it was a high point for a reason, a gorgeous, sad melody, with Mariah's voice working off and around the harmonies of Boyz II Men, over the keyboard work of Walter Afanasieff, who, it seemed, would be her partner in some ways forever. It was the kind of song to resonate with anyone who'd ever lost someone, but without ever being a dirge, and a strong indicator—as was everything on this record—of the way Mariah's writing had grown.

If anything, "Open Arms," the Journey song, seemed out of place here. Although it brought back memories for Mariah, the song itself was rather overblown. Thankfully, she and Walter had toned down the arrangement, but it still somehow sounded too glossy, particularly coming after the very heartfelt "One Sweet Day." And even the added background vocals of Melonie Daniels and Kelly and Shanrae Price, with their gospel edge, couldn't save what had never been a very good tune. Still, as missteps went, it was a small one, one track that didn't live up to the excellence of all the others.

"Always Be My Baby" lightened the mood considerably. The rhythm was still a little downbeat, but the changes had a warm feel, and Mariah's vocal almost purred over the top. Indeed, on much of this record, she sounded slightly different from the Mariah of old, a little sassier, a little more R&B, like a soul sister. And it wasn't someone playing a wannabe, either; this was in her blood and was gradually coming out. Her love of soul, gospel, R&B, and hip-hop all fed into it. While not quite a slow jam, the song had a lush, sexy vibe that just glowed.

From there, the album moved to the closest it would come to gospel, "I Am Free." With Loris Holland on Hammond organ behind Walter's keyboards and programming—Holland had helped out on *Merry Christmas*—the gospel feel was perfectly genuine and unforced, an indication that Mariah wasn't abandoning her roots by any means. However, her writing and arranging were both becoming more sophisticated, as the lines of the chorus seemed to cascade into each other, something a less technically gifted vocalist would have had trouble singing, but which seemed just right coming from Mariah.

Mariah was slowly moving away from the "standard" ballad, and edging slowly toward territory that seemed more Toni Braxton than Celine Dion. It suited her, but ballads had been her bread and butter, her stock-in-trade, since *Mariah Carey,* and she wasn't about to abandon them completely. Nor did she need to. "When I Saw You," cowritten with Walter, showed she hadn't lost her touch. About love at first sight, it rang with hope, and offered a reminder of just how powerful her voice could be when she chose to unleash it.

From there, it was a quick return to hip-hop/R&B territory with "Long Ago," where Mariah let her voice slide like silk over an insistent bassline. Her second collaboration with Jermaine Dupri and Manuel Seal in writing, arrangement, and production, it could easily have been *Daydream*'s fourth single, with a nagging chorus and a sliding instrumental hook.

But "Melt Away," which Mariah had written and performed with Babyface, by now a massive star in his own right, could just as easily have served as that single—but it never happened. A gorgeous slow jam, it lived up to its title, as the two voices really did melt into each other, after Mariah's low "Barry White" introduction. It was curious that Mariah produced this track alone, given Babyface's pedigree at the controls; but, there was no denying that she'd done a superb job, as the song glided into its chorus, as strong as any jam released in the nineties, and one that would find a lot of favor late at night with dancers.

Stylistically, "Forever" was something of a throwback, bringing up memories of fifties ballads in its chord changes and in the way guitar arpeggios stayed at the forefront of the music. In many ways, the song harkened back to the feel of Mariah's first album, but with a richness to the voice and the sound that she hadn't been capable of then. In that regard, then, it seemed a shame that, compared to the best songs on *Daydream*—which were very good indeed, with Mariah continuing to take giant steps—"Forever" came across as something of a throwaway.

And that made it odd that the album's real throwaway, "Daydream (Fantasy Sweet Dub Mix)," had so much life to it. Mariah had brought in David Morales, best known for his club mixes, to help remix "Fantasy" into something quite different, something that brought to mind dub music, with elements dropping in and out of the mix. The result was something quite adventurous, with Mariah's voice being just one element (and not necessarily the main one) in the musical stew. Its sights were quite firmly set on the dance floor, and in those terms, it succeeded, a declaration of intent that Mariah was expanding her horizons. Dance music in particular, but also hip-hop, had changed beyond recognition in the last few years, becoming much more a part of mainstream culture. When Mariah made "Dreamlover," Walter had been unfamiliar with the technique of using loops; now, it was common practice. Hip-hop ruled the charts, R&B was decidedly radio-friendly, and the dance revolution had spread across the country. Mariah was familiar with it all. She listened avidly to the radio, took it all in. And, at twenty-five, she was young enough to be a part of it all, something she wanted to be, a member of her own generation, not someone isolated and timeless, which had seemed to be where Columbia had wanted to put her after *Music Box.*

Even Mariah's ballads had an edge, and the closing cut on *Daydream,* "Looking In," moved into far more personal territory than anything she'd done before. This was as naked as she'd let herself appear on record, the accompaniment suitably stripped down, as she reflected on her life now, the changes she'd gone through, and the difference between the public perception of Mariah Carey and the real person. Intimate and revealing, it made an appropriate end to the album, and was evidence that Mariah was growing, changing, and becoming much more herself, confident of who she was and what she could do. As she explained in *Vibe,* "I sometimes defer to people who've had more experience. That was my motto for a long time. But now I'm able to say, 'I don't agree with you.' Now if I don't do what I want, I'm the only one to blame."

Was Mariah now in the position she really wanted to be in, or was she still an artist in transition? With *Daydream,* she'd definitely changed the face of her music, turning it toward R&B, and a sound that was more contemporary than classic. But it was a process that had begun with *Music Box,* albeit very tentatively. "Dreamlover" had dipped the tip of a toe into the water, and she'd obviously been pleased with the result. *Daydream* saw her up to her knees. It was a record that could appeal to a new audience, but without going so far as to lose the fans who'd fallen in love with her for her "classic" sound. But this wasn't a case of hedging her bets. Her roots were in soul, gospel, even hip-hop, but also in pop. It all meant a lot to her, and out of it, Mariah was learning to create something that was uniquely hers. She was getting there, bit by bit; where she went from here would prove to be very interesting indeed.

11

W here Mariah went was a place not many had expected her to go: she started her own record label. Her aim was not to release her own records—she was very firmly contracted to Columbia, and had no wish to change that—but to run a label herself, under the auspices of Sony, which would give her excellent distribution.

She'd spent a lot of time talking to people at Sony about it, and planning everything. The label, which she'd christened Crave (although she would never reveal why), was set to become operative during 1996. In many ways, it would be a vanity project, not unlike Madonna's Maverick label, which was distributed through Warner Bros. However, it would also be a viable commercial entity. "I want to discover new talent that otherwise would end up nowhere," she said. "I know exactly how it feels to have a tape and not to have anybody listening to it seriously. I had a lot of luck. I was there at the right moment. For a lot of upcoming talents it is very hard to get in touch with the important people."

The first act Mariah signed was a hip-hop duo from Queens, New York, called Blue Denim, which included Kimberly ("Kimmie Kat") James, the younger sister of Salt'N'Pepa's Cheryl James. Immediately, Mariah was working with them in the studio, writing and singing hooks on a few tracks, on an album that would be released in the fall of 1996. But it would be early 1997 before Crave achieved its first chart hit, when the single "Head Over Heels," by the all-female R&B group Allure cracked the *Billboard* Hot 100.

"I'm trying to work with any of the artists who want my input or want help or want to collaborate," Mariah told Fred Bronson.

"And it's cool for them because I'm a peer. I reached success at an early age and it's easy to relate to me as a friend, not just a record company person."

But a label wasn't the only thing on the horizon as 1996 began. There was the small matter of a few concerts around the world, principally in Japan and England, and the awards she'd been nominated for, including two American Music Awards nominations and a remarkable six Grammy nominations (and an appearance on the awards show, singing "One Sweet Day" with Boyz II Men).

Daydream had obviously had a major impact on the awards committees. But it was the American Music Awards that provided the greatest gratification, as Mariah won the award for favorite female artist in both the Pop/Rock and Soul/R&B categories; for someone who was just beginning to see herself as an R&B singer, this was heartwarming indeed.

It was certainly better than the Grammy show. After her performance, Mariah spent the rest of the evening in her seat, passed over time and again in every category in which she'd been nominated, as Joan Osborne and Alanis Morrissette walked away the big winners of the evening. "What can you do?" she'd say later. "Let me put it this way. I will never be disappointed again. After sitting through that whole show and not winning once, I can handle anything. But—and I know everyone always says this—I wasn't expecting to win."

However, she didn't let the losses get her too far down. Once the show was over, the parties began, and although there were reports that Mariah spent the entire time in a corner, sulking, that simply wasn't the case. In fact, she said emphatically, "I actually had a great time there and was one of the last to leave. I practically closed the joint."

There was little time to reflect on the disappointments, however. Mariah—who'd been officially acknowledged as the "World's Best Selling Recording Artist" at the World Music Awards, with a total of 80 million records—was about to leave for her dates in Japan.

When the tickets had gone on sale in January for three shows at the Tokyo Dome, with its 50,000 seats, every one was sold within three hours, breaking the gate receipt record for the venue, which had been held by the Rolling Stones.

As the anticipation for Mariah's arrival and her shows grew, Japan found itself in the grip of Mariah mania. There were articles and pictures everywhere. She was even covered on the national news! *Merry Christmas* became Japan's all-time top-selling album, only to be surpassed a few weeks later by *Daydream.* (This would give Mariah four of Japan's top five all-time best-selling albums.)

Of course, she had been quite visible in Japan for a while. In 1994, Sony had made her its "image girl" in a MiniDisc advertising campaign. And "All I Want for Christmas Is You" had been the theme song for a very popular Fuji TV Christmas drama. Then, to coincide with the tour, Mariah's face began appearing in lipstick ads for her own brand, manufactured by the Japanese cosmetic company Kose (one of the sponsors of Mariah's Japanese dates).

The concerts—on March 7, 10, and 14—were spaced apart to allow Mariah's voice to recover from each show. "It's very strenuous to sing all my songs back to back," she explained. "But," she added, "I'm actually really looking forward to it."

Mariah's warm-up for this date had been about as big as it was possible to get—a sold-out show at Madison Square Garden during the fall of 1995. It was a one off show, partly to celebrate the release and immediate success of *Daydream,* but mostly to prepare Mariah and her crew for Japan. And it also provided the opportunity for another home video, *Fantasy: Mariah Carey at Madison Square Garden,* again directed by Lawrence Jordan.

It might have been Mariah's second concert video—amazing for a performer who'd only played a handful of live shows—but it was more relaxed and upbeat than her last outing. This was immediately apparent when Mariah took the stage clad in the pants and shirt she'd worn for the album cover and went straight into "Fantasy."

She was accompanied by the people who'd become her live

musical core: Dan Shea on keyboards, Vernon Black on guitar, Randy Jackson playing bass, Gigi Conway on the drums, percussionist Peter Michael, and music sequencing by Gary Cirimelli. All were under the direction of Walter, while Kelly and Cheree Price, Melonie Daniels, and Cindy Mizelle provided backing vocals. It was a crew that was used to each other, that worked well together.

The concert offered a selection of material old and new, with the emphasis on tunes from *Daydream.* Mariah was joined by Boyz II Men for a glorious version of "One Sweet Day," and then Wayna Morris took Trey Lorenz's part for "I'll Be There."

Perhaps the biggest surprise to everyone came at the end of the concert, however, when Mariah left the stage after "Vision of Love." The Puffy remix of "Fantasy" began to play over the P.A., and Ol' Dirty Bastard was suddenly onstage, rocking the house with his rap, as images from the video flashed on the screen.

All in all, the concert was a huge success, giving Mariah the chance to air her vocal chords in public. And for someone whose performances had been limited, she seemed remarkably at ease in such a big place, working the crowd, establishing a rapport. There was even a snippet on the video from the Fresh Air Fund benefit she'd done the year before at St. John the Divine, with Mariah singing "Joy to the World," as well as footage of Mariah at Camp Mariah, talking to the kids. And, to round things off nicely, there was also the video for "One Sweet Day."

And now Mariah was ready for Japan.

Everything reached fever pitch on March 7, as Mariah took the stage in Tokyo for the first time. Japanese audiences had a reputation for being reserved, but they quite openly adored her. For Mariah, though, it was nerve-racking at first. "First of all, you're in front of so many people that basically don't speak your language," she said on MTV's "Week in Rock," adding "It took a little getting used to, but I think by the end of the show, you know, everybody started to kind of relax." She even managed to rouse the crowd enough to sing along to "Always Be My Baby."

The stage show, which took as its basis the Madison Square Garden concert that had been edited down for the *Fantasy* home video, began with "Daydream Interlude (Fantasy Sweet Dub Mix)" as the dancers moved around onstage, setting the scene for Mariah's entrance, and her first song of the evening, "Emotions." Then she went into two ballads, "Forever" and "I Don't Wanna Cry," before lightening the mood with "Fantasy" and "Always Be My Baby." Then, as she changed costumes, the background singers got a chance to shine on Chaka Khan's "Ain't Nobody," before Mariah reemerged to perform "One Sweet Day," with the video backdrop of Boyz II Men from the Madison Square Garden show. After that, she sang "Underneath the Stars," "Without You," and "Make It Happen," before going into her second cover song of the evening (one she hadn't recorded, but had used on her previous American tour): the SOS Band's "Just Be Good to Me." Then it was "Dreamlover" and the dancers' turn in the spotlight, as the "Fantasy" remix played, and the video was shown on the giant screens that flanked the stage (ensuring that everyone could see Mariah). The final section of the show began with "Vision of Love," building through "Hero," to climax with "Anytime You Need a Friend," which went straight into its Clivilles and Cole remix version.

And then it was over, and the lights went up. Mariah had performed fourteen songs, as much as her voice could stand in one evening. The show had been very much a "Best of Mariah," but that was perfectly understandable; these people had waited six years to see her, and they wanted to hear the hits that had made her so famous. It was as if she was obliged to perform them, and she did.

HER WORLD TOUR would cover a lot of territory, but not too many shows. After Japan came a break, quite a long one, until the late spring and early summer—late May and June—when she toured Europe, playing England, France, Holland, and Germany. And that was it. By the end of June, her commitments were complete, and Mariah was able to rest and begin thinking ahead to her next record. For her, it was never too early to be doing that, even though she had no plans to enter the studio before January 1997.

So the remainder of 1996 saw her writing, working in her home studio in Bedford, and thinking. Thinking about her life. Success could seem like an end in itself, and Mariah was continually surrounded by the rewards of everything she'd done: the awards, the platinum records, even the house itself, which she and Tommy had spent a reported $10 million on, splitting the cost right down the middle.

She was beginning to have an inkling, however, that something in her life wasn't the way she wanted it to be. Everything *seemed* idyllic, almost as if her life was charmed, but that was simply on the surface. Deeper down, Mariah wasn't happy. As usual, she'd be staying up all night, working until 7 A.M. Or if she was spending time in the city, she'd be out, hanging out at clubs, hearing the latest music.

She could sense the changes happening in herself. She was ready to have her music move even more radically toward R&B and hip-hop for her next record, but according to sources, Columbia wasn't too happy about that. When she'd done the "Fantasy" remix with O.D.B., she said, "Everyone was like, 'What are you, crazy?' [Columbia is] very nervous about breaking the formula. It works to have me sing a ballad on stage in a long dress with my hair up." While Columbia president Don Ienner, who'd been involved with her career at Columbia from day one, said he'd been "incredibly positive" about the remix, he did admit that "There might have been some [who fought it]."

But the remix worked. Not only did it garner a lot of press, it was incredibly popular, proving Mariah right. And she was realizing that the girl who'd built her career on ballads had grown up, had become a sensual woman. The big ballads no longer represented her quite the way they once had done. It was a change that had been happening gradually, but it was definitely there. Now she was, by her own definition, "R&B."

"She gets in her car, puts on her radio stations, and it's always R&B," said Walter Afanasieff. "She knows every song, every word, every rap out there."

As the year progressed, Mariah found herself taking on a number of different writing partners for her upcoming project. There was Walter, of course, but also people like Missy ("Misdemeanor") Elliot, who was just starting to hit it big; Cory Rooney (who also happened to be in charge of Black Music at her Crave label); and Stevie J. She'd even been talking to Sean ("Puffy") Combs about having him produce one of the album tracks, as opposed to just a remix. This time out, she was going to fully show her colors. "I'm not this one-dimensional girl who sits in a field wearing a flannel shirt or stands onstage singing only ballads," she insisted. "And I feel I'm in a better position to express myself at this point."

According to some, Tommy preferred her singing ballads. Perhaps it was something that illustrated the eighteen-year age gap between them. Perhaps it was his personal taste. It made for an odd situation, albeit one they'd always managed to work out. He was her husband, and ultimately her boss. But she was one of his star attractions.

By January 1997, Mariah was ready to record, eager to get into the studio, a place that, over the last few years, had been virtually a home to her. But at the same time, that feeling gnawing at her made her want to try something new. In earlier interviews, she'd always denied wanting to get into movies, but now she started acting lessons, five days a week, with renowned New York coach, Sheila Grey. In some ways, it worked as therapy, giving her a chance to return to some of the rocky terrain of her childhood. "It's been an incredible release for me," she admitted. "I would come out of sessions emotionally drained, because I was getting in touch with all this stuff that I'd never really dealt with—even things from my childhood." One moment of revelation came when Grey asked her to return to a place in her life where she'd felt safe and "I didn't have one. I couldn't think back to a place that didn't give me a feeling of shakiness or some negative memory."

Whether the acting lessons were the catalyst, or whether something had been building for a long time and finally reached a head, on May 30 Mariah and Tommy announced their separation. To those who'd said from the very beginning that they were an unlikely match, it was time to rub hands gleefully as their predictions came true. In reality, however, it was a sad time; there's never joy to be found in the end of a marriage.

Immediately, rumors began to fly about the causes. Some charged that Tommy had been nothing less than a control freak, refusing to let his wife have handsome men in her videos, not wanting her to wear the tight, sexy clothing she loved, even monitoring her calls at home.

Supposedly, in December 1996, Mariah had begun spending more and more of her time in Manhattan, rather than Bedford, using New York studios to do all her pre-production work on her new album, and living in hotels. There were also unconfirmed rumors floating around that she'd begun an on-and-off affair with New York Yankees shortstop Derek Jeter, whom she'd met at a benefit for the Fresh Air Fund in November. A few went so far as to cite this as *the* cause for the breakup.

Naturally, there were cynics who believed that Tommy had married Mariah both as a trophy and as a ticket to greater success for his label, and those who felt she'd wed him as a way to further her career.

All this, however, was nothing more than speculation and innuendo. But it was generally agreed that Tommy hadn't wanted the marriage to end, and that Mariah had done her utmost to make it work. "She gave it a million percent," one friend commented.

Many factors can strain and break a marriage. It was quite possible, in this case, that the age difference and the difference in tastes had something to do with it. And the mix of personal and business situations couldn't help but complicate any other issues. Mariah was twenty-three when she married, and still had a lot of growing to do. Her childhood might have been hard, but for the most part, her adult years had been insulated, hidden away in recording studios. She hadn't had a chance to spread her wings and truly discover herself. Perhaps in Tommy she saw the father figure who had never really been present in her life.

Whatever the reasons, with the announcement, the marriage was largely over after a little less than four years. Both Mariah and Tommy had stayed largely quiet about the causes. They hadn't been the ones assigning blame and firing salvos at each other. Instead, they'd taken the high road of silence. But no matter what they said or didn't say, the rumors would have flown, anyway; that was the nature of the world.

And silence was all for the best in more ways than one. Tommy had signed a new contract with Sony that would keep him in his position for another five years, and Mariah still owed the company five albums, which meant they'd be working together for quite a while. Acrimony wouldn't have served either one of them well. "I love Tommy, and he will always be a part of my family," Mariah said in an interview with Elysa Gardner in the *Los Angeles Times.* "There's absolutely no bitterness between us. The best thing I could hope for would be to have a great friendship with him, because he is someone I respect and admire and look up to in many ways. But right now, it's my time to grow as an independent woman."

And that, if the tabloids were to be believed, meant being seen out with all manner of men. Besides Jeter, Mariah was linked with Sean ("Puffy") Combs, rapper Q-Tip from A Tribe Called Quest, and even Boyz II Men's Wayna Morris, the two having apparently fallen for each other during his birthday party at the Metrodome in New York. There were also rumors that she was partying with gangsta rappers. Not long after the rumors appeared in print, Mariah's application to buy a Manhattan apartment in a co-op building was turned down by the board. "It was ridiculous," Mariah said. "There were rumors and lies about me being the next queen of gangsta rap, which did not help."

And, she admitted, the press attention she was receiving was unlike anything she'd known before. "I've never had to deal with this before, because I've never been out there in this way. All of a sudden, [journalists] are like, 'Whoo! Here she goes! Stop the presses, she's goin' wild!' . . . The fact is, I end up collaborating with more men than women in my work, and I form friendships with most of the people that I work with. But that doesn't mean that I'm sleeping with all these guys! I'm not!"

In truth, the last thing Mariah wanted was to go into another relationship. "I have a lot of trust issues," she admitted in *Cosmopolitan.* "I don't know if there's anybody whom I fully trust. And I don't need to sleep with, like, one hundred guys to make up for lost time. If I'm with somebody, it's going to be because I really love him, not because I feel the need to go wild."

She'd made the personal break from Tommy, although she'd never had any intention of leaving Columbia—for one thing, she was legally tied there. To signal the start of a new life, a new Mariah, she also parted company with her manager, Randy Hoffman, and her attorney, Allen Grubman. Her new manager would be Hollywood dealmaker Sandy Gallin, who was based on the West Coast.

So, ONE PART of the fairy tale ended.* But that didn't mean that Mariah's life as Cinderella was over. As a singer, she'd been going from strength to strength, discovering herself, widening her musical horizons. If anything, the future looked more promising than ever before.

---

*And it ended completely in March, 1998, when Mariah flew to the Dominican Republic to obtain a "quickie" divorce. Now she was truly free again.

12

The public got its first taste of the new, freer Mariah when the video for "Honey" premiered on MTV. As it was meant to do, it turned heads. Suddenly, Mariah was grown up, Agent M, very sexy, showing a lot more of herself—in more ways than one: in action escaping from a mansion, riding a jet ski while evading the pursuing thugs, and ending up on a beach safe in the arms of a hunk. This was, for the first time, Mariah as a babe.

Not only that, but the music was different. "Honey" went all the way into hip-hop, further than Mariah had ever gone before, thanks to Puffy being at the controls. Apparently, he had been given a free rein to do his magic—magic that had already produced two consecutive number 1 singles, "I'll Be Missing You" and "No Money Mo Problems."

The idea for the video had been entirely Mariah's. "[It] was my whole concept," she said. "[Director] Paul [Hunter] and I talked about it for a while, and collaborated on it." Shot during the summer in Puerto Rico, "It was a grueling process; I'm not going to say it was easy. I got up at 3 A.M. every day, and worked until 9 in the morning the next day—for four hours in a row, swimming in my Gucci pumps! I can't say that I really jumped off the roof, but [I did] dive into the pool. But I did wear and swim in those pumps, and I was not happy."

It all seemed innocent enough, another video with a story line, plenty of spy overtones, and action. But there were people eager to read a lot more into it, a subtext of Mariah escaping the controlling grip of Tommy Mottola. Even Walter Afanasieff, who was loyal to both Mariah and Tommy (his employer), called it "the most incredibly coincidental thing that you could put out. Everything in the video is 'F**k you, Tommy.' "

Mariah, however, insisted that that simply was not the case. There was no slight to Tommy intended in the video, and the people who thought there was were just imagining things. Even so, a few insisted that the video was a parody of the way she'd been treated.

And what was Tommy's reaction? "Tommy loves the video," a spokesperson said, "and says it's the best yet from Mariah."

With its clothes and sensuous looks, it was certainly racier than any video she'd made before.

"I don't really think the video is overtly sexual," Mariah contested. "But for me—I mean people used to think I was the nineties version of Mary Poppins!"

Whether the "Honey" video was controversial or truly innocent was irrelevant to most of the people who watched it on television. Or to those who rushed out the week of the single's release and gave Mariah something that had never been achieved before—her third single to enter the *Billboard* Hot 100 at number 1.

Its importance went well beyond its chart placing, however. "Honey" was the record that gave Mariah hip-hop credibility. Before that, she'd been seen as a pop singer with R&B tendencies, someone who might have liked hip-hop, but who wasn't really a part of that scene. "Honey" changed that perception, and even those who'd once dismissed Mariah as a wannabe were forced to take a second look.

To be fair, a good deal of this success had to do with Sean ("Puffy") Combs's production, but the song had originated with Mariah, after she'd worked with rapper Q-Tip, from A Tribe Called Quest. "[They] had an idea and they asked me to come in and produce the record," Combs said. So far it seemed so good. But he wasn't allowed in the studio when Mariah was doing her vocal takes—an odd situation for a producer. "A lot of people feel I'm overbearing," Combs explained, so I wasn't allowed [there].

I'm trying to work on that. I'm such a perfectionist, sometimes I don't give people the chance to breathe. . . . Mariah [recorded "Honey"] until she thought it was perfect, like a hundred times. She gave me a hundred tracks to choose from."

The combination of Mariah and Puff Daddy seemed to be magical, and there was no denying "Honey" had exactly what the charts were looking for, even if it seemed like a fairly radical departure for Mariah from the music for which she was known. But it was really the product of a woman who now felt in a position to express herself more freely. With its samples of "The Body Rock" by Treacherous 3 and "Hey DJ," on top of Q-Tip's drum programming, Stevie J's keyboards, and additional vocals from Mase and The Lox, this was a Mariah no one had had a chance to hear before: very sexy, very sassy, very contemporary. Like all of Combs's productions, "Honey" sounded dense, but there was a lot of space within the sound.

"I don't know where I got the idea about honey and love, but I like it," Mariah said.

This hit not only made her the first artist to have three singles go straight in at number 1, but it also gave her the most number 1 hits of any female solo artist—twelve—one ahead of both Madonna and Whitney Houston. And it put her in a fourth-place tie with the Supremes for the most number 1 singles, behind only Michael Jackson, Elvis, and the Beatles. She was now in very prestigious company. And, essentially, it made her a classic pop-era singer, not that she wasn't one already.

"Honey" only lasted at number 1 for two weeks, but somehow that didn't matter. Its impact had been made, and the "new" Mariah had been announced. So when her album *Butterfly* appeared on September 16, it too entered the chart in the top position.

"My songs have never been this personal before," Mariah said, and one glance at the lyric sheet emphasized the truth of that statement. Musically, not everything on *Butterfly* was as drastic a move toward hip-hop as "Honey," but nevertheless this didn't seem like the same Mariah who'd made *Music Box*. There were ballads, with the title track Mariah's "absolute favorite," which she called "the best ballad I've ever written." But even the ballads were lean, sinewy, and strongly weighted to R&B. And it was very notable that one of them was dedicated to Tommy.

For the up-tempo tracks, Mariah had widened her range of collaborators. She seemed to have her finger on the pulse of music, picking people who would become very hot, like Puff Daddy and Missy ("Misdemeanor") Elliot, with whom she cowrote "Baby-doll."

"Mariah, she listens to rap," Elliot said. "She's straight up just cool."

On remixes of "Honey," there would be raps from Da Brat and Mase, while "Breakdown" would find Wish Bone and Krayzie Bone from Bone Thugs-N-Harmony rapping. This was the album of someone way into hip-hop, not a wannabe. All the money in the world couldn't buy this kind of credibility.

"I started the album last January [1997] and finished early August," Mariah explained in *Jet*. "But, I did three videos in between [as well as "Honey," she made videos for "Breakdown" and "Butterfly," the last of which she'd also directed]. This album is definitely something I've wanted to do for a long time. There were songs I wanted to do in the past. I recorded them, but they never got on the album. That happened even on the first album because some people felt they were too R&B or whatever the terminology was. It's been a gradual process of my being able to say that this is what I'm doing to do at this point. People owe it to you to let you express yourself. With all the changes that I've gone through both professionally and personally, it was a release to work on the album." For the first time, she'd really thrown her caution away, and that made this album particularly gratifying, "because it's something that I feel fully responsible for and because I took chances."

It wasn't just "Honey" that was getting widespread airplay. "Breakdown" was being widely requested, as was "Butterfly," particularly after the video Mariah conceived and directed began hitting heavy rotation on the music channels.

If it seemed odd, at least part of her inspiration came from the "weird dreams" she'd had after taking melatonin to help her sleep. In one dream, she'd been chasing something that leapt a barbed-wire fence. Mariah had tried to follow, but couldn't, and cut her finger on the wire. "I didn't put the blood in the video. Too gory."

Butterfly gave new grist to the critical mill, but the acceptance that had begun with *Daydream* seemed to more or less continue, albeit rather halfheartedly. Writers seemed to want to point out Mariah's split from Tommy, noting its impact on her lyrics, now that she was a "free woman" again.

"Fans will . . . find *Butterfly* full of the kind of glossy, richly decorated love tunes that shimmer when illuminated by Carey's bright voice," noted David E. Thigpen in *Time,* pointing out, "It continues the evolution that Carey began on *Daydream*—away from pure pop toward a keener-edged R&B and hip-hop influenced sound." He felt this was a much more adult record: "Underneath its cool sheen runs a thread of insecurity and loneliness that gives *Butterfly* a richer, more mature outlook."

In *Entertainment Weekly,* David Browne found her a slightly unconvincing R&B queen, simply because of the "penthouse-culture setting" that was her lifestyle. He was willing to concede, though, that she was moving toward R&B, but she was "caught between old and new habits and taking cautious baby steps into the future."

Overall, the record didn't convince him. While it was "pleasant," he felt that "Carey's attempt at musical maturity ends up backfiring. The very-slow-jam grooves have an intimacy lacking in her previous work. But the arrangements—especially the oozing vocal harmonies on many tracks—mute the impact of the lyrics. . . . [T]he most distinctive tracks on *Butterfly* are still its gushy, sky-high ballads."

While it was true that there were out-and-out dance tracks on the album, that had never been Mariah's intention. Hip-hop had largely moved away from the freneticism of Public Enemy to catch a groove that was more laid-back, a groove that suited Mariah's voice perfectly. Whether or not the critics accepted it, those involved in hip-hop did, and most importantly, so did the fans, the final arbiters of what was good or bad. If they hadn't liked the album, they wouldn't have gone out by the millions and bought it, quickly sending it to triple platinum in the United States and to number 1 in Japan.

The release was celebrated, not with a concert, but with a rare public appearance by Mariah, who autographed copies of the disc at Tower Records, at Sixty-sixth Street and Broadway in New York. Crowds lined the street overnight to have the chance to see her. The day before, she'd been on Oprah Winfrey's show, singing "Butterfly" and "Hero," and on November 12, she'd be the musical guest on "Saturday Night Live" (just as she had been when *Mariah Carey* appeared), singing "Butterfly" and "My All." And on September 16, came the "official" launch of the record, with a party at New York's Pier 59 Studios.

Butterfly was, without doubt, more focused than anything Mariah had done before. And, as she'd wanted it to be, it was an R&B album. Even the ballads she'd written with Walter, fully half the record, had a sound that definitely leaned in that direction.

Butterfly started off, as Mariah's albums tended to, with the first hit single, "Honey." Beyond question, this was a hip-hop track, driven by Q-Tip's drum programming and Stevie J's keyboards, all lined up behind Mariah's voice (although longtime cohorts Melonie Daniels and Kelly Price would add some background vocals throughout the album), and a production—by Puffy, with a little help from Mariah—that managed to be both dense and airy. This went beyond anything she'd done in the past. It was street hip-hop music, with a booming bass, built around samples of "The Body Rock" and "Hey DJ." But it was also pop, with a catchy chorus, combining hip-hop and pop into one for something that simply wasn't going to be denied by anyone, and offering a powerful start to the record.

"Butterfly," the next song, more than lived up to the promise.

Mariah had described it as her favorite, and the best thing she'd ever written, and it was easy to hear why. Cocomposed with Walter, who, with Dan Shea, handled all the instruments, it was very personal, and different from any ballad she'd written before—richer, sexier, more grounded in the R&B she loved, but without any traces of gospel influence (indeed, there'd be none of that on *Butterfly*). As it was meant to, it soared.

"My All," another collaboration with Walter, took Mariah deeper into the territory she'd explored with Babyface on her last album. The surprise, really, was that Babyface hadn't been involved with the song. The sound, the lushness, even the style seemed to have his marks. But Mariah and Walter wrote, arranged, and produced the whole thing themselves. Even the guitar arpeggios were not quite real, sampled then played on the keyboard. But "My All" succeeded; it had the kind of slinky, slow-jam R&B sound that Toni Braxton had once made her own, and it fit Mariah like a glove.

Then the bpm increased a little for the groove of "The Roof." Incorporating bits of "Shook Ones" into its sound and produced by Poke and Tone with Mariah, it had been composed by Mariah with a number of others, including Cory Rooney, who contributed keys. Lyrically, this was some of her best work ever, the melody slinky and overtly sexy, confirmation—as if any was needed by this point!—that this was a new Mariah.

"Fourth of July," another ballad cowritten with Walter, was as close to the old Mariah as *Butterfly* came. And even this was jazzier than she'd been in a long time, much closer to, say, "Vanishing" or "The Wind" than to "Hero." But even then, it was less straightforward, with more of a swing and even a touch of sass.

The next two tracks, "Breakdown" and "Babydoll," were, perhaps, the album's backbone, its real declaration of independence. "Honey" stood at one extreme, while some of the ballads stood at the other. Pure R&B, these songs occupied the middle ground. "Breakdown" saw Puffy and Mariah behind the boards again, with guest raps from Wish Bone and Krayzie Bone from Bone Thugs-

N-Harmony, who also helped out with the backgrounds. Like "Honey," "Breakdown" showed Mariah treading forcefully into territory that was new for her and making it her own; it had a melody that simmered under her vocal, and a groove that was irresistible.

"Babydoll" teamed Mariah with yet another writing partner, Missy Elliot. "I had the hook already," Mariah explained, "as well as a melody and lyric for the chorus. Then she and I collaborated on a new melody for the verses, and we did the first verse, and the second half of the second verse together." Unlike much of the album, which was recorded in New York at Mariah's Crave Studios or The Hit Factory, or even at WallyWorld in California, Walter's home base, much of "Babydoll" came together in Atlanta, where Missy lived. This had a bonus, since it helped reunite Mariah with an old friend who lived there—Trey Lorenz, who added to the background vocals. "Babydoll" was a vocally driven piece, as sensuous as Mariah was likely to get, with a sparse arrangement kicked along by some inventive drum programming by Cory Rooney.

Following these came two ballads, "Close My Eyes" and "Whenever You Call," which, while up to the standard of anything Mariah had done before, suffered in comparison. But even here you could hear the new Mariah in the spareness of the arrangements and the way it was her voice, rather than any instrument, that controlled the song. She'd grown to the point where having less behind her really proved to be more, for the song and for her. It was notable, too, that like the other ballads on the record, these two leaned very much toward R&B.

"Fly Away (Butterfly Reprise)"—essentially *Butterfly*'s "Fantasy (Sweet Dub Mix),"—was a chance for David Morales to take the tune apart, and for Mariah and him to create something new out of it. This included adding some lyrics from an old Elton John song. "[I]t's like a twist on the original record," Mariah said. "Actually, when I wrote 'Butterfly,' I had a house record in mind, but then I started thinking about it while writing it, and it turned into a ballad. But I had to do the other one too, so they're both on the album." This gave them a chance to explore the original possibilities of the song, and it did kick along to a thumping house beat, propelling some inventive keyboard and vocal work, showing yet another new facet of Mariah.

After that, it all quieted down again for a cover of Prince's "The Beautiful Ones" with Dru Hill. This wasn't a reprise of "One Sweet Day" in any way, but a homage to one of Mariah's favorite artists, done with the help of one of the best R&B groups around. Voices slid into each other, showing how simple, but how good and how effective the song was. And while it might not have added anything to the original, it did offer a lovely vocal outing.

It all came to a close with "Outside," a ballad Mariah had written with Walter. Interestingly, for the first time on one of the ballads, they added a third person in the control room, Cory Rooney, who added to the song's feel. Spare, pleading, this was Mariah stripped to the basics, lyrically and musically, finishing it all as she'd started: stronger, prouder, a new woman, a natural woman who'd come into her own.

13

The year 1997 had been one of drastic change for Mariah, culminating in huge personal success. She'd even been asked to contribute (and had given an unreleased version of "Hero") to the Princess Diana Tribute album. But 1998 would be her busiest year yet. It was as if she was bound and determined to plunge headlong into her career.

The year certainly started with a number of high notes. Mariah was nominated for an American Music Award—and won—for Favorite Female Artist in the Soul/R&B category. The Blockbuster Entertainment Awards had her nominated for Favorite Female–Pop for *Butterfly*. Then came her nomination in the 29th NAACP Awards, for Outstanding Female Artist, a recognition that she was, in part, black. And finally, to finish out the first week of the year, came nominations for the Grammys, for Best Female Vocal Performer, Best Female R&B Vocal Performer, and Best R&B song. Sadly, once again she'd walk away from the Grammy, empty-handed.

It was an auspicious way to begin a year, and it had to be gratifying for Mariah that some of the nominations were in the R&B categories, given that R&B had been her aim with *Butterfly*.

But there was barely time to consider any of this. Since before Christmas, Mariah had been in intense rehearsals for what was her first truly big tour. It began January 11 in Tokyo, where she played the first of four sold-out dates (the others were January 14, 17, and 20) at the Tokyo Dome. Tickets went on sale the month before, and all 200,000 had been snapped up within an hour. From Tokyo, she crossed to Taiwan, playing Taipei on January 24, and then she moved to Australia for a series of shows. There was Brisbane on January 30, then two concerts in Sydney on February 3 and 6, Perth on February 10, and then two dates in Melbourne on February 13 and 16. Finally, the Asian leg of the tour concluded in Honolulu on February 21. The twelve shows were the longest stretch Mariah had ever undertaken live, even though it lasted more than a month. After that, she took a break, and during the summer and fall she'd tour Europe and America. By the standards of most singers or bands, the tour seemed incredibly long, with too much time between shows, but Mariah knew her voice and the way it reacted to being on the road. To give the fans what they wanted, she had to treat her vocal cords carefully, and she was determined to do so.

But the tour was only one of her commitments for the year. The acting lessons she'd taken had paid off, and Mariah was set to follow in the footsteps of Whitney Houston, Madonna, and Janet Jackson and make a movie, which had been written for her. "It's set in the seventies, the soul music era," she explained. "I feel it's a whole different outlet for me. Who am I playing? That's for you to find out. I've kept one song back for the soundtrack, which is a ballad."

Mariah was, it seemed, just beginning to realize her potential. Over the course of six albums (although *Merry Christmas* perhaps doesn't count as a "real" album, being more a side project made for the fun of it), she's shown a remarkable growth—musically, of course, but also as a person. In some ways, it's hard to connect the self-assured woman of *Butterfly* with the girl who made *Mariah Carey* in 1990. Eight years have seen so many changes—marriage, separation, riches beyond her wildest dreams—and they've been reflected in her songs.

Mariah has been one of the most prolific of contemporary singers, which is all the more remarkable considering she's been responsible, either as writer or cowriter, for virtually all her material. Her work ethic has been tremendous. And all the time, she's kept her finger very closely on the public pulse. It's as if she's known what people will want to hear. Of her singles, only five have failed to reach number 1, and her worst performance has been number 12, a remarkable record. She's had more number 1 hits than any other solo female singer, and only eight fewer than Elvis, the all-time leader. She's become one of the best-selling artists in the history of music. And when you remember that she's accomplished all this in less than a decade, it puts her achievements into perspective.

Love her or loathe her (and she certainly has her detractors), there can be no denying that Mariah Carey is *the* contemporary artist. No one during the 1990s has come close to her kind of success, or touched so many people around the world. She's truly in a class by herself, and really, she's just begun. At twenty-eight, she has several decades as a professional singer ahead of her.

In the future, however, it seems as if singing will be only one of Mariah's activities, although it will certainly remain her main one. She's always wanted to act, and now she'll have the opportunity. She's produced her own records, and worked with other acts, as well as composing for them, and she'll certainly expand her involvement in those fields as time passes. In every way, the future for Mariah is wide open. In a few years, there's a good chance she'll fall in love and marry again. Quite possibly, she'll have children and a home life that will fill a lot of her days; she's already said that if she ever does have children, she wouldn't want them raised by a nanny.

There will be other female singers who'll come along in the future. Some may even eclipse the records Mariah has set. But her place in the musical history books is already assured, not only for the number of hits and total record sales, but also for the music she's created, and the effect it has had on the people who've heard it. And it's music she'll continue to create, for many years to come.

Whatever fads rise and fall, and whatever artists come and go, there will only be one Mariah Carey.

DISCOGRAPHY

SINGLES (all on Columbia)

		Chart No.
Vision of Love	(1990)	1
Love Takes Time	(1990)	1
Someday	(1991)	1
I Don't Wanna Cry	(1991)	1
Emotions	(1991)	1
Can't Let Go	(1991)	2
Make It Happen	(1992)	5
I'll Be There	(1992)	1
Dreamlover	(1993)	1
Hero	(1993)	1
Without You/Never Forget You	(1994)	3
Anytime You Need a Friend	(1994)	12
Endless Love (duet with Luther Vandross)	(1994)	2
Fantasy	(1995)	1
One Sweet Day	(1995)	1
Always Be My Baby	(1996)	1
Honey	(1997)	1

ALBUMS

Mariah Carey	(1990)	1
Emotions	(1991)	4
MTV Unplugged	(EP) (1992)	3
Music Box	(1993)	2
Merry Christmas	(1994)	3
Daydream	(1995)	1
Butterfly	(1997)	1

HOME VIDEOS

Mariah Carey: The First Vision	(1991)
MTV Unplugged + 3	(1992)
Mariah Carey	(1993)
Fantasy	(1995)

AWARDS

Grammy Awards	Year
Best Pop Vocal Performance	1991
Best New Artist	1991

American Music Awards

Favorite Soul/R&B Female Artist	1991
Favorite Pop/Rock Female Artist	1993
Top Contemporary Album	1993
Favorite Pop/Rock Female Artist	1995
Favorite Pop/Rock Female Artist	1996
Favorite Soul/R&B Female Artist	1996

"Soul Train" Awards

R&B/Urban Contemporary New Artist	1990
R&B/Urban Contemporary Single, Female	1990
R&B/Urban Contemporary Album, Female	1990

Billboard Music Awards

Hot 100 Singles Artist	1991
Top Female Album Artist	1991
Top Female Single Artist	1991
Top Female Album Artist	1992
Top Female Single Artist	1992
Female Artist of the Year	1994
Special Chart Performance Award	1996

New York City Music Awards

Best Female Pop Vocalist	1991

Rockefeller Center Awards

Award for worldwide sales of more than 20 million copies of *Music Box*	1994
Award for worldwide sales of more than 55 million records since 1990	1994

World Music Awards

America's Best Selling Recording Artist   1995
World's Best Selling Recording Artist   1996

UK Smash Hits Awards

Best Female Solo Singer   1994
Best Female Solo Singer   1995

Bravo Magazine (Germany)

Best Female Artist   1994

Australian Record Industry Association Awards

Most Popular International Album of the Year   1994
Take 40 Australian Best Chart Album Performance   1994
Most Popular Solo International Female   1994

For those interested in contacting Mariah Carey or in joining her fan club,
the address is:

Mariah Carey Fan Club
PO Box 679
Branford CT 06405

The fan club can also be reached via their website at:
http://www.mariahcarey-fanclub.com
Two other official websites of interest are the Official Sony site, where fans
can subscribe to an email list:

http://www.sony.com/Music/ArtistInfo/
MariahCarey/ butterfly__flat.html
and Mariah Carey Echoes:
http://www.ellipsiiis.com/mariah/